PRAISE FOR *HE HEARS HER VOICE*

In my life, the prayers of my mother were profoundly critical to the foundation of my life in ministry. They rescued me from doubt and rebellion as a teenager and set me on a life path of ministry I never could have imagined. Candy Marballi's book reminds me of the impact of those fervent prayers. Candy captures the essence of such praying. Her thoughtful testimonies and personal reflections, along with practical biblical insights, will inspire and equip you to make just such a profound difference through your daily prayers. Embrace this prayer covenant, apply it to your daily life, and stand amazed at the impact you can have as a mighty woman of prayer!

Dick Eastman
International President, Every Home for Christ
President of America's National Prayer Committee

The lives of millions of children globally have been encouraged as a result of Candy Marballi's leadership in prayer. I am grateful that the ministry of The Prayer Covenant partners with Cru and The Jesus Film Project in a number of locations.

Now, Candy's release of *He Hears Her Voice* seems especially timely with so many people facing challenges beyond their control. I pray God will use this resource to influence significantly more women to develop a lifestyle of effective, powerful prayer.

Steve Douglass
President Emeritus, Campus Crusade for Christ/Cru

Candy Marballi is a dear friend who, together with her husband, Vik, encourages the biblical mandate of praying for one another. This beautiful devotional calls women to pray for one another! Queen Esther requested prayer and fasting as she faced the king on behalf of her people, the Jews, at a time of great crisis. Today, we can follow in her footsteps as we face unequaled challenges, keeping in mind that the One we pray to loves us, and as we pray according to His will, He hears us. We are to God the sweet aroma of Christ, just like the exquisite flower on the cover of this book.

Luis & Doris Bush
Servants of the Most High God

He Hears Her Voice is a global gift for God's daughters in any walk of life. Candy's evident joy and passionate love for God will inspire and challenge you to first covenant with Jesus Christ then invite others on the journey with you. Engaging biblical passages, intriguing personal stories, anointed hymns, and personalized prayers will entice you to move through the pages of this book in one sitting. Don't do it! Day by day, take time to soak in His presence, express your praise, pour out your petitions, and live in the abundance the Father desires for you. Whether you are a seasoned intercessor or beginning prayer, you will discover this is a treasure that cannot be kept to yourself. It must be shared with others!

Kay Horner
Executive Director, Awakening America Alliance

He Hears Her Voice comes at a time when prayer is much needed throughout the world. This is a timely call for women, God's daughters, to covenant in prayer and go boldly before the Almighty Father to lift up all our petitions and requests. Deeply relatable biblical passages, vivid personal stories, power-filled hymns, and inspiring prayers are used to contemplatively guide the reader into a powerful covenant with God and our neighbors. For the woman who has always wanted to start the habit of prayer but didn't know where to begin, this covenant will help you establish that intentional rhythm of prayer in your life and open up the doors of spiritual blessing that only spending time with God can unlock and unleash.

Lisa Pak
Director of Global Engagement, FTT, Saddleback

Sometimes as life gets busy and the world seems to spin out of control, I feel a desperate need to reignite a vital connection with God. Do you ever feel that way? This beautifully crafted book beckons you to a quiet place to read, reflect, listen, and share your heart with the One who gives life, light, and hope. Through worship, prayer, study, and application of His Word, Candy leads women to enter into a holy communion with our Lord. There is no time like now to strengthen your personal prayer life and unite your heart in prayer with women all around the world!

Laura Fisher
Senior Vice President, Global Ministry, Biblica,
The International Bible Society

Candy Marballi is a woman with a mission. She has helped children worldwide engage with God from an early age through *The Prayer Covenant for Children*, a fully illustrated teaching guide that has been translated into many languages. Now Candy has produced a multifaceted, powerful prayer guide that will ignite and deepen your daily walk with your heavenly Father. Each brief and spiritually arresting chapter includes relevant passages of Scripture, stirring prayers, pungent questions, and compelling action steps for ten five-day sequences.

I commend *He Hears Her Voice* to both women and men. You will be encouraged, motivated, and uplifted to take this unfolding spiritual journey with these two vibrant women of God. I love what Candy wrote: "When we spend time in the presence of Jesus, intentionally praying all He desires for us, we experience answers to prayer.... Whether it is a few minutes or hours, prayer is life-giving and fills us with hope because we are in the presence of the greatest hope-giver."

John Robb
Chairman, International Prayer Council

I first met Candy Marballi while she was writing *The Prayer Covenant for Children*. Soon after, she attended the 4-14 Window Global Forum in New York to share her new book with children's advocates from around the world. Leaders from different countries immediately responded with enthusiasm, as they saw the book's potential to disciple children into a lifestyle of prayer. I later encouraged Candy to join a global mission forum to share more about her ministry and about *The Prayer Covenant for Children*, and the results were the same: new friendships and ministry partnerships were born in just a couple of days.

More recently, Candy became the newest member of the International Prayer Council leadership team; and again, the same thing happened. Friendships and ministry partnerships began blossoming around the world. Candy is a friend-magnet and the Prayer Covenant is proof positive. Just ask any of the millions of children from more than fifty nations who are using *The Prayer Covenant for Children*. They'll tell you it's true!

Here's my caution to you: If you are content with your current prayer life, be careful. Because if you read and apply the message of her new book, *He Hears Her Voice*, it will change your life. And there's a very good chance you will make a few more friends as a result.

If you are in for an adventure, and if you love God and want to grow in your relationship with Him and with others, then go for it! *He Hears Her Voice* is for you. Candy is one of my closest friends, and she keeps introducing me to new friends all the time. Who knows? Maybe one of them will be you.

Tom Victor
President, Great Commission Coalition

I believe God will use *He Hears Her Voice* to bless His people and multiply the impact of The Prayer Covenant with women around the world. Candy Marballi is a leader among leaders. She is highly respected for her love for the Lord and for children and has responded to this call by developing *He Hears Her Voice*.

In this book, Candy systematically presents each line of the prayer, developing it with clarity and depth. She provides suggested memory verses, probing questions, and specific action steps. This book will inspire a new thrust forward among women of faith who believe God's promises and are growing in their love for and discipline of prayer. Praise God!

Jerry Kirk
Founder, The Prayer Covenant

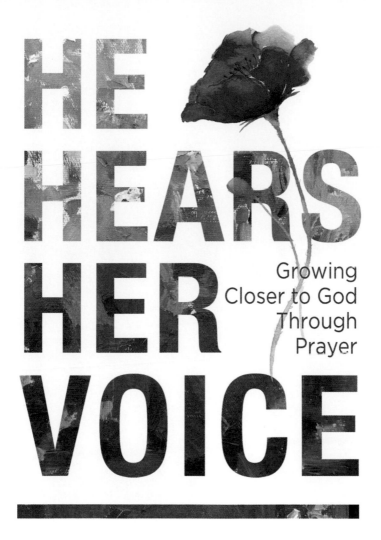

HE HEARS HER VOICE

Growing
Closer to God
Through
Prayer

Candy Marballi

Ellie
Claire

New York • Nashville

Ellie Claire
Hachette Book Group
1290 Avenue of the Americas, New York, NY 10104
ellieclaire.com

First Edition: April 2022

Ellie Claire is a division of Hachette Book Group, Inc. The Ellie Claire name and logo are trademarks of Hachette Book Group, Inc.

The publisher is not responsible for websites (or their content) that are not owned by the publisher.

Unless otherwise noted, all Scripture references are from The Holy Bible, New International Version®, NIV® Copyright © 1973, 1978, 1984, 2011 by Biblica, Inc.® All rights reserved worldwide.

Scripture references marked NKJV are taken from The Holy Bible, New King James Version®. Copyright © 1982 by Thomas Nelson. Used by permission. All rights reserved.

Scripture references marked TLB are taken from The Living Bible copyright © 1971 by Tyndale House Foundation. Used by permission of Tyndale House Publishers Inc., Carol Stream, Illinois 60188. All rights reserved. The Living Bible, TLB, and the The Living Bible logo are registered trademarks of Tyndale House Publishers.

Print book interior design by Bart Dawson.

Library of Congress Cataloging-in-Publication Data
Names: Marballi, Candy, author.
Title: He hears her voice : growing closer to God through prayer / Candy Marballi.
Description: First edition. | New York : Ellie Claire, 2022. | Includes
   bibliographical references.
Identifiers: LCCN 2021041687 | ISBN 9781546000679 (hardcover) | ISBN
   9781546001591 (ebook)
Subjects: LCSH: Christian women--Religious life. | Prayer--Christianity. |
   Spiritual life--Christianity. | Spirituality--Christianity.
Classification: LCC BV4527 .M258 2022 | DDC 248.8/43--dc23
LC record available at https://lccn.loc.gov/2021041687

ISBN: 978-1-5460-0067-9 (hardcover)

Printed in China

APS

10 9 8 7 6 5 4 3 2 1

To the One who "delivered my soul from death,
my eyes from tears, and my feet from falling."

PSALM 116:8 NKJV

CONTENTS

Foreword

BY REV. LISA PAK

Now is always the time to pray. In these challenging days, we know this in our heads, but it's often hard to find the space in our hearts, minds, souls, and schedules to do so. When the time crunch comes, prayer is the first to go, even though we honestly intend to connect with God later. And this is exactly why this book is so timely.

Candy and I met through prayer. When I joined Finishing the Task (FTT) just as the COVID-19 pandemic took over the world, Candy's name was mentioned several times as someone I had to get to know because she prays—and she prays with passion, fullness of heart, enduring perseverance, and confident expectation. And prayer is what we need as FTT, under Rick Warren's leadership, looks to the Great Commission task of the twenty-first century. But let's be honest, we all need prayer. Not just for the grand visions, but for everyday life. There is so much that steals our time, and we can literally feel the stress of packed schedules, competing commitments, unexpected changes, and all the accompanying anxieties encroaching upon our peace. We are unsettled. We need to pray.

Prayer is an essential part of the sacred rhythm of the peaceful mind, unworried heart, and unhurried spirit. Candy has written this book for all the women who have put everyone and everything else before their own soul-care. For all of God's daughters who feel like their voices are silenced and not heard, this book is a reminder that the Living God hears the cries and inclines His ear to the prayers of His daughters. Drawing from the Bible, personal testimonies, spiritual readings, and hymns, Candy will take you through the practice of building a lifestyle centered on and rooted in prayer. As you take in the words, let them percolate and know that this prayer book is a covenant for you. God deeply desires to covenant with you. God hears your voice, and He longs for you to hear His.

Rev. Lisa Pak

MDiv, MABL, Gordon-Conwell Theological Seminary

DMin Student, Tyndale University '22

Global Strategist, Finishing the Task

Introduction

I n the following chapters, we will uncover the ten themes
that comprise this simple prayer. Each theme includes
five days of activities, including memory verses, study
and reflection, inspiring stories from women around the
world connected with the Prayer Covenant ministry,
meditative psalms, worship songs, a closing prayer, and
application. The prayer itself takes about one minute to
pray, but oh, what power is unleashed once prayed!

The heart and soul of the prayer covenant is to pray for
others, every day by name for an agreed number of days.
When we promise to pray for another, it shows not only
our love for them but our willingness to be accountable
to another as we follow Jesus more intimately with them.
Begin with one and as God leads, continue to add more for
whom you are praying. This level of commitment deepens
your relationship with Jesus and with one another. It's
wonderful for husbands to pray with wives; parents with
their children or grandchildren; friends with best friends or
those with whom you may have shared Christ and whom
you want to encourage.

Set aside time each day—morning is best, before
your day begins—to pray the prayer and meet with Jesus.
Grounding your day in prayer assures you of His presence
throughout your day. As David wrote in Psalm 108:1–3,
"My heart, O God, is steadfast; I will sing and make music

with all my soul. Awake, harp and lyre! I will awaken the dawn. I will praise you, LORD, among the nations; I will sing of you among the peoples." Morning prayer is also emphasized in Psalm 5:3, "In the morning, LORD, you hear my voice; in the morning I lay my requests before you and wait expectantly." In Mark 1:35 we see Jesus doing the very same thing with His Father.: "Very early in the morning, while it was still dark, Jesus got up, left the house and went off to a solitary place, where he prayed."

Create a special prayer space for yourself to meet Jesus each day. I love to pray with worship music in the background and near a window. Choose whatever space offers a peaceful, restful and worshipful environment that you look forward to each day.

The Daily Prayer has ten themes:

Grace is foundational. We learn to identify God's grace in our own lives thereby helping us share His grace with others.

Love helps us understand we were created to be loved by God, to love Him in return, and to share His love with others.

Compassion is the second half of the Great Commandment. It means loving people and learning how we can be most effective in living out the commandment to love others as Christ loved us.

Repentance talks about the holiness of God and how He cannot hear or answer our prayers if there is unrepentant sin in our lives. It also stresses the importance of forgiveness and how Christ demands we forgive others or we will not be forgiven.

Worship is focused on whole-life worship—not just songs we sing in church.

Commitment is the crux of the prayer covenant. It involves total surrender to the Lordship of Jesus Christ in our lives.

Dependence acknowledges that we cannot love like Jesus, show compassion like Jesus, be forgiving or committed like Jesus without the power of His Holy Spirit working in and through us.

Influence invites the reader to be intentional about asking God to open up opportunities to make a difference in the lives of those over which we have influence.

Discipleship challenges us to make Jesus' last command—to go into the world and share the gospel—our first priority.

Authority gives us confidence to boldly approach God's throne with these ten unshakeable truths, knowing this changeless God, who spoke creation into being, who parted the Red Sea and was victorious over death itself, possesses the authority and power to answer our prayers.

This Bible study has been designed purposely to be light on the homework and heavy on simply resting, worshipping, and enjoying being in the presence of Jesus, the living God. Our lives today are so hurried, stress-filled and demanding, if we rely on our own strength, we will burn out and be crushed under the daily pressures of life.

Don't rush through the themes. It is designed to be used Monday through Friday; one activity each day. But if you need to combine a few days to fit your schedule, do what works for you.

Day 1 introduces the theme, the daily prayer, and offers an inspiring story with questions.
Day 2 allows you to reflect on the theme with a beautiful Psalm.
Day 3 invites you to reflect on the theme with a hymn or song of worship.
Day 4 takes you deeper into God's word with commentary and questions.
Day 5 concludes the theme with a closing prayer and application.

There may not be a more beautiful expression of showing our love for Jesus and for one another than prayer. When we pray, we give ourselves fully to Jesus. We trust Him to accomplish great things in and through us. We recognize His sovereign authority. When we spend time in the presence of Jesus, intentionally praying all He desires for us, we experience answers to prayer.

What a privilege we have to approach God's throne in prayer! Paul shares, "Since the day we heard about you, we have not stopped praying for you" (Colossians 1:9). Prayer covenants, as I'll explain more fully in the next chapter, are a wonderful way to pray effectively for others. They are an invitation to see the power of God in and through your prayers; to experience powerful answers and transformation. Prayer covenants invite the Holy Spirit into your prayer time as you commit to praying His will over yourself and those for whom you pray each day. Whether it is a few minutes or hours, prayer is life-giving and fills us with hope because we are in the presence of the greatest hope-giver.

Call to me and I will answer you and tell you great and unsearchable things you do not know (Jeremiah 33:3).

If you remain in me and my words remain in you, ask whatever you wish, and it will be done for you (John 15:7).

THE PRAYER COVENANT
FOR WOMEN PRAYER

Dear Heavenly Father,

Grace
Thank You for loving me and making me Your daughter.

Love
Help me love You with my whole heart.

Compassion
Help me love others the way You love me.

Repentance
Thank You for washing away my sins and making me clean.

Worship
Help me rejoice in You always in spite of my circumstances.

Commitment
I want to follow You as my Lord and Savior.

Dependence
Fill me with Your Holy Spirit. Make me a woman after Your own heart.

Influence
Make me an instrument of Your grace, truth, and justice.

Discipleship
Use me for Your glory and to be a blessing to others.

Authority
Gracious Father, I pray in the name of Jesus Christ our Savior and in the power of the Holy Spirit. Amen.

How to Use This Book

Though we are surrounded by a "do it yourself" culture, this book is not about going it alone, but about the rich experience gained by following Jesus together. My suggestion is to begin with one person—possibly a close friend or spouse. Later you can include more family members or Bible study friends. Invite the Holy Spirit to guide you to whom you should invite into a covenant and when.

The prayer you read on the previous page is designed especially for women, based on the same ten themes as the original Prayer Covenant developed by Jerry Kirk. The themes are important. They speak of God's character, challenge you to make Jesus the Lord of your life every day, empower you by His Holy Spirit, and equip you to share His message with those around you. The prayer is easy to use. I know some individuals who pray it for over one hundred people on their prayer list, alone. Others awake and partner with another in the wee hours of the morning. It's up to you when and how you put this prayer to use!

You do not have to pray the exact lines. God will guide you and pray His prayers through you as you embark on this prayer journey.

There is no required set number of days for your prayer commitment. There is freedom in how many days you choose to partner in prayer with a friend, group, or loved one. Many choose thirty days or forty days. Establishing a set number of days offers a natural way to end a prayer journey with someone and begin with someone new. The importance is accountability: knowing you are indeed praying for a particular person by name—your spouse, child, loved one, friend—whomever God has led you to partner with in prayer. We also have a Prayer Covenant for Children that families enjoy using together, as they pray for one another.

A prayer commitment empowers discipleship, transformation, and evangelism. When you daily pray through its ten themes—grace, love, compassion, repentance, worship, commitment, dependence, influence, discipleship, and authority—it instructs your heart. This leads to transformation. The more time we spend with Jesus, the more we become like Him—which results in evangelism—and desire to share His love with those we meet.

So press on and pray on, *together*.

CHAPTER 1

GRACE
The Good Shepherd

MEMORY VERSE

For it is by grace you have been saved,
through faith—and this is not from yourselves,
it is the gift of God—not by works,
so that no one can boast.

EPHESIANS 2:8–9

Definition of Grace

Unmerited divine assistance given to humans
for their regeneration or sanctification

PRAYER

Dear Heavenly Father,
Thank You for loving me and making me Your daughter.
Help me love You with my whole heart.
Help me love others the way You love me.
Thank You for washing away my sins and making me clean.
Help me rejoice in You always, in spite of my circumstances.
I want to follow You as my Lord and Savior.
Fill me with Your Holy Spirit. Make me a woman after
　　Your own heart.
Make me an instrument of Your grace, truth, and justice.
Use me for Your glory and to be a blessing to others.
Gracious Father, I pray in the name of Jesus Christ our
　　Savior and in the power of the Holy Spirit. Amen.

STUDY

As you begin the study, carefully read the definition of
grace, pray the daily prayer, and review your memory verse.

Grace is unmerited; we do not deserve it. We are
unworthy to receive it, and that's what makes it so
amazing. We begin to understand God's amazing grace

only when we recognize our unworthiness, our sin, and our inability to measure up to a holy God. Grace exchanges doubt and despair for hope and life. God's grace says, "You are worthy. I made you in My image for My purposes. I love you." Grace means being loved even when you didn't do anything to deserve that love.

Jesus, "the Lamb of God, who takes away the sin of the world" (John 1:29), graciously extends His love and grace to you and me.

In our daily lives, we all have met people who were grace-filled as well as those who didn't have a deep understanding of grace. Maybe we see grace when watching someone's response to a senior who keeps asking the same question again and again. Perhaps it is a parent's response to a child who is continually crying for attention. Or maybe it is simply someone's response in a difficult situation.

Grace takes form and shape in our hearts and lives. As followers of Christ, we are invited to partake of His extravagant grace and to share it freely with others.

Grace lays the foundation for this study because we cannot be channels of God's grace to others if we ourselves lack an understanding of grace.

The following is a story of such grace—how a young girl growing up in a village in China met the Lamb.

NAOMI'S STORY

I love the Lamb. I always have. I can remember so clearly the first day I saw Jesus.

I was quite young…maybe six or seven. I was living with my grandmother in a small Chinese village where no one goes. I'm so thankful someone went.

He came from England, or so it was rumored among the village folk. My grandmother had heard he was in town…we all knew he was in town, as he would sing and dance in the streets to attract the children who would follow him. Where would they go? I had no idea, but Grandmother made it very clear, I was not to follow him… ever! "He'll take you away and tell you strange stories about other lands and will take you from our gods. Don't you ever go with him."

Well, I did. I didn't mean to. I dearly loved my grandma, but the temptation became too much for me that day while I was washing dishes. Grandma was sleeping, and I heard the sound. It was simple, it was subtle, and at first, I didn't even realize it was him, but as he and his little followers passed near our house, I caught a glimpse of him. He was dancing and singing a song, inviting the children— the dirty, poor children—to join him. He looked so odd with his pale complexion and reddish hair. He was the first foreigner I had ever seen, yet he looked so friendly, so fun.

Curiosity got the best of me, and since Grandma was taking her afternoon nap, I decided to go for it. I slipped out of the house and quickly ran to join the other kids parading after this intriguing figure.

He led us to a small little hut, where he had us sit down and spoke to us in his funny, broken Chinese. I was intrigued by his words. They were unlike any I had ever heard before. He spoke of things I had never heard in our temples, or by our priests and elders. He said two things that I would never forget and would change my life.

"There is a God in heaven who created you. He loves you, and has sent His Good Shepherd, Jesus, to save you, hold you, comfort you, lead you, and bring you home."

A God in heaven who knows me? The One who created me cares for me and loves me? I had never heard of such a god, and it touched my tender spirit.

And then I saw the lamb. This foreigner gave each of us a piece of paper with an outline of a shepherd holding a little lamb. I joyfully joined the other children in coloring the drawing. However, about halfway through, when I remembered my grandmother and the fact that I wasn't even supposed to be there, I jumped up, ran back to the house and back to my dishes. Grandma was still fast asleep.

About ten minutes later, I heard a knock on the door. To my surprise, several of the kids who were with me in that dusty hut were standing in front of me. "He wants to see you," they said.

"No, I wasn't even supposed to be there! My grandma had forbidden me from even going! Why does he want me?"

They shrugged their shoulders and said firmly, "He told us to come get you."

As I returned, I was shocked that the foreigner was holding my unfinished drawing in his hands. "Is this your drawing?" he asked. I could only nod my head. "It's very good. I see you colored all the sheep around the shepherd, but you forgot the one he is holding."

I mustered up all my courage to respond. "That's the pure little lamb," I said meekly.

"Oh," he mused, "…that's right! Would you like to be the Good Shepherd's little lamb, too?"

I nodded. Then, I recall him placing his huge, calloused hands on my head and praying over me. I had no idea what he was doing. No idea what I was supposed to do, but I knew, then, two things:

I knew there was a God in heaven who had created me and loved me.

I knew there was a Good Shepherd, Jesus, who would comfort and guide me.

In my remote village there were no churches, no Christians, no Bibles…no one to teach or disciple me. For ten years, I only knew there was a Creator God, and a Good Shepherd named Jesus.

One quiet night it all changed. I was having a terrible time sleeping alone in my room at university. An overwhelming sadness came over me. I kept tossing in my bed. Suddenly, I heard a voice. "Do you remember Me?" I was stunned. No one was in the room. I got up to check. I eventually assumed it must have been my imagination. When I got back in bed, I was about to lie down, when I heard it again, this time even clearer, "Do you remember Me?"

Suddenly, the image of that drawing of the shepherd when I was seven years old appeared right in front of me. I could see the little lamb nestled in his arms. I began to weep. "The Good Shepherd?" I whispered.

"Yes," He said, "it's time to serve Me."

The next morning, as He directed, I found a small fellowship of Christians meeting on my university campus. To my amazement, there was another missionary, sent from Canada. He was training this group of young Chinese youth. I was eager to begin my journey and thankful God had sent someone to disciple me.

I came to believe in God and His Good Shepherd, Jesus, when I was seven years old, from that man whom I never saw again. But I began to serve Him at seventeen. I have not stopped and have no intention of ever doing so.

QUESTIONS

1. What does grace mean to you?

....
....
....
....

2. How was grace illustrated in Naomi's story?

....
....
....
....

3. Can you describe a recent situation when you received unexpected grace and how you might be a channel of God's grace to those around you?

....
....
....
....
....
....
....
....

DAY 2

A Psalm

REFLECTION

The Psalms have been my go-to in every stage of life. I have found great comfort, encouragement, and wisdom within each chapter. I've read and reread all 150 psalms countless times, and each time I have discovered new insights and nuggets of profound truth. Some are more precious than others. I often find myself praying Psalm 91 or 139 over our children. Psalm 145 is my favorite psalm for intergenerational worship. There could be no more perfect psalm for our Good Shepherd story than Psalm 23.

PSALM 23

The Lord is my shepherd, I lack nothing.
He makes me lie down in green pastures,
he leads me beside quiet waters,
he refreshes my soul.
He guides me along the right paths
for his name's sake.
Even though I walk through the darkest valley,
I will fear no evil,
for you are with me;
your rod and your staff,
they comfort me.

You prepare a table before me
in the presence of my enemies.
You anoint my head with oil;
my cup overflows.
Surely your goodness and love will follow me
all the days of my life,
And I will dwell in the house of the LORD
forever.

When the sea of life is raging and swirling around you, simply pray, "Lead me beside still waters." When you feel burdened and overwhelmed by the circumstances of life, pray, "Make me lie down in green pastures." When all seems dark and desperate and discouragement sets in, or when depression raises its ugly head, cry out, "Restore my soul!" And the Good Shepherd will hear and answer you because He is good and faithful and full of grace. One of my favorite Bible verses is found in Jeremiah 33:3: "Call to me and I will answer you and tell you great and unsearchable things you do not know." He gives us permission to cry out any time, any place, anywhere.

In the psalm above, highlight in RED what speaks to your heart. Highlight in YELLOW what God might be inviting you to do. Highlight in BLUE God's promises.

Hymn of Praise

REFLECTION

Music enriches my worship time with the Lord. I've always loved music and appreciate all forms of worship. The classic hymns are doctrinally rich, and their lyrics will be scattered throughout these chapters.

Saddleback Worship has written and performed some of the most beautiful praise and worship songs I know. I am grateful they have allowed us to include some of them in this book.

It is a blessing in this digital age that we can put a song title into our search engines and enjoy a time of praise and worship. Whether you choose to read and meditate on the words, sing along with a recording, or worshipfully dance to the music, bask in the knowledge that you are dearly loved. Your debt has been paid, your guilt completely removed, all because of the marvelous grace of our loving Lord and Savior, Jesus Christ.

ROOM AT THE TABLE
2017, Saddleback Worship

I can come just as I am
You welcome me, You welcome me

I can lay my burdens down
You carry me, You carry me

With love in Your eyes You ran, and
With grace in Your voice, You said

There is room at the table
There is room at the table
When I'd wandered so far,
You came after my heart
You made a way and
Set a place for me
There is room at the table

You took me in and made
Me Yours when
You called my name, You called my name
Greater love
I've never known
You took my place, You took my place

You traded Your life for death
You rose from the grave and said

There is room at the table
There is room at the table
When I'd wandered so far
You came after my heart

You made a way and
Set a place for me
There is room at the table

There is nothing
You would not overcome
There is no one
Who can stand in Your way
There is nowhere
I could hide from Your love
Your mercy never fails
Your mercy never fails

There's always room, always room
There's always room
Always room

Digging Deeper

STUDY

Jesus loved telling stories and understood the power of a good story. He drew crowds and captivated audiences. I sometimes close my eyes and imagine what it must have been like to sit in the grass and listen to Jesus. When He walked this earth, He wanted those who listened to engage their senses and use their imaginations. Imagine being in the room where the woman wept and worshiped as she anointed Jesus' feet with precious perfume, ignoring the disapproving glares from the other guests at the table. Think how the prodigal felt being met with open arms as he ran toward his father, or picture being a disciple on the rough seas when they thought they would perish.

Whatever the story or event, we can truly experience all Jesus intended when we engage our senses—imagine smelling the sea air, hearing Jesus' reassuring words when He commanded the sea to calm in the midst of the storm, or touching His feet and smelling the fragrant perfume that had been poured over them. That is how the Bible can come alive for each of us.

Apply all your senses as you read Luke 15:3–7. This

will help you use your imagination to experience the story on a deeper level, and discover its hidden meanings.

> Then Jesus told them this parable: "Suppose one of you has a hundred sheep and loses one of them. Doesn't he leave the ninety-nine in the open country and go after the lost sheep until he finds it? And when he finds it, he joyfully puts it on his shoulders and goes home. Then he calls his friends and neighbors together and says, 'Rejoice with me; I have found my lost sheep.' I tell you in the same way there will be more rejoicing in heaven over one sinner who repents than over ninety-nine righteous persons who do not need to repent."

Here you see Jesus leaving the ninety-nine sheep to go and look for the one that was lost. What a powerful reminder that Jesus pursues us! Even when we stray, Jesus cares deeply and wants to rescue us. He has His Father's heart: full of compassion and rich in mercy. Jesus is looking to save all those who are lost. He is graciously extending His invitation for everyone to experience an abundant life found only in Him. Why?

> Because He is "not willing that any should perish" (2 Peter 3:9 TLB).

Because He's come to "seek and to save that which was lost" (Luke 19:10 NKJV).

Because He is the Good Shepherd who "gives His life for the sheep" (John 10:11 NKJV).

Because "he chose us…before the creation of the world to be holy and blameless in his sight…. He predestined us for adoption to sonship through Jesus Christ…to the praise of his glorious grace" (Ephesians 1:4–6).

Because we are God's "special possession…called…out of darkness into his wonderful light" (1 Peter 2:9).

And because "He who did not spare his own Son, but gave him up for us all…will…graciously give us all things" (Romans 8:32).

Reread Psalm 23. I was recently convicted while reading this psalm. It was as if a spotlight magnified the words: "The LORD is my shepherd, I lack nothing." The poignant imagery of Jesus as our Shepherd in Psalm 23 brings assurance—because the Lord is our Shepherd, we lack nothing. No matter how much or how little we may have in this life, if we know Jesus, if He indeed is our Shepherd, we can say with confidence: I lack nothing!

Whatever situation we may face, we have the assurance that He will walk with us through the darkest valley, the most painful relationship, or the biggest challenge because He is Jehovah Rohi, our Shepherd. He is the Lover of our souls, our Comforter, our Teacher, and our Guide, and we are His forever.

> Because of His grace, Jesus guides me along the right paths for His name's sake.
>
> Because of His grace, I am afraid of nothing because Jesus is with me.
>
> Because of His grace, Jesus prepares a table before me in the presence of my enemies.
>
> Because of His grace, He anoints my head with oil.
>
> Because of His grace, my blessings overflow.

Jesus loves us lavishly! We are daughters of the Most High God, and He withholds no good thing from those who love Him.

The all-sufficiency of God's grace is why we can say with confidence, "I lack nothing." Paul reminds us in 2 Corinthians 12:9, even during times when it may feel like we lack everything, God's "grace is sufficient for you" because God's "power is made perfect in weakness." In the midst of pain, God is with us. In the midst of injustice, God is for us. Whatever battle we are facing, whatever hardship, rest assured that God the Father is with us.

When we recognize the depth of our own sin and find forgiveness, freedom, and newness of life in the person of Jesus, we begin to understand the profound gift of grace.

As our memory verse reflects, "By grace [we] have been saved.... Not from [ourselves], it is the gift of God" (Ephesians 2:8). We must come to God as little children, completely dependent upon His mercy, His atonement, His sacrifice. It's all about Him.

Jesus is inviting you to experience His pleasure, His passion, His love for you. As you close your eyes, take hold of His hand—His nail-scarred hand—and let Him lead you beside still waters, and restore your soul. He is the Good Shepherd who takes great delight in you, who quiets you with His love, and rejoices over you with singing (Zephaniah 3:17).

QUESTIONS

1. How is grace demonstrated in the story of the lost sheep?

. . . .

. . . .

2. When Jesus found the lost sheep, what did He do?

. . . .

. . . .

3. Is there something you are lacking in your physical, spiritual, or emotional world?

....

....

4. Have you gone to Jesus, the Good Shepherd, and asked for His help? His divine intervention? Do you believe He wants to help you? Why or why not?

....

....

5. Write down whatever you need in the lines below. Ask God to graciously supply your need.

....

....

6. How does the knowledge of Jesus rejoicing over you make you feel?

....

....

7. What's your favorite passage on grace? Commit it to memory.

....

....

....

DAY 5

PRAYER

O precious Jesus, Lover of my soul,

You are Jehovah Rohi, the Good Shepherd, who has given Your life for me on Calvary's cross, who ran after me when I wandered away, who called me by name, and who made room at Your table for me. I bow before You in praise of who You are. Thank You for Your grace that has made me Your dearly loved daughter. Thank You for Your mercy and loving-kindness. Thank You for Your faithfulness that is new every morning. Thank You for guiding my steps. I ask that You lead me, O Lord, beside the still waters. Restore my soul. Lead me in paths of righteousness for Your name's sake. Fill me with joy and peace. Make me a channel of Your love and grace to my family, friends, and all those around me. Give me opportunities to speak of Your greatness and glorious splendor. Shine in and through me this day.

In Your name, the name above every name, I pray. Amen.

ACTION STEPS

1. What makes grace so appealing to you?

....
....
....
....

2. How will you apply this lesson in your daily life?

....
....
....
....

3. With whom and how will you share this truth?

....
....
....
....
....
....
....
....
....

CHAPTER 2

LOVE
A Mother's Cry

MEMORY VERSE

See what great love the Father has lavished on us,
that we should be called children of God.

I JOHN 3:1

Definition of Love

Unselfish, loyal, and benevolent concern
for the good of another

PRAYER

Dear Heavenly Father,
Thank You for loving me and making me Your daughter.
Help me love You with my whole heart.
Help me love others the way You love me.
Thank You for washing away my sins and making me clean.
Help me rejoice in You always, in spite of my circumstances.
I want to follow You as my Lord and Savior.
Fill me with Your Holy Spirit. Make me a woman after
*   Your own heart.*
Make me an instrument of Your grace, truth, and justice.
Use me for Your glory and to be a blessing to others.
Gracious Father, I pray in the name of Jesus Christ our
*   Savior and in the power of the Holy Spirit. Amen.*

STUDY

As you begin the study, carefully read the definition of *love*,
pray the daily prayer, and review your memory verse.

   God's love is a steadfast, perfect, and pursuing love.
His love is in us, through us, and over us. How can it be
that the overwhelming love of God stays with us even

when we try to run from it? He relentlessly pursues us with a never-ending, forever, and always kind of love. The Lord is gracious and compassionate and rich in love. Paul says it this way in Ephesians 3:17–19:

> "I pray that you, being rooted and established in love, may have power, together with all the Lord's holy people, to grasp how wide and long and high and deep is the love of Christ, and to know this love that surpasses knowledge—that you may be filled to the measure of all the fullness of God."

It is not easy to comprehend God's love for us, but when we do, we overflow with His fullness and His love will overflow. We will see ourselves as He sees us and see others as He sees them. We crave God's unconditional love because we were designed for it.

AILEEN'S STORY

In 1963, my mom, Aileen, was in a hotel room all alone, pregnant with me, crying out to Jesus to show her that He was truly the Messiah.

Aileen was born to Jewish parents. She met my father and had married him by the time she was sixteen—with her parents' approval. There was one stipulation. Since my father was Italian (his parents came from Sicily and settled in New York City), he was asked to change his name from Caruso to Carr before my grandfather would grant permission. That was easily done.

My dad made a good living and supported my mom and older siblings in style, but he wasn't fully satisfied. One night the electricity went out. My father turned on a battery-operated transistor radio and for the first time heard the Gospel. When Billy Graham gave the invitation, my father immediately responded and accepted Christ as His Savior. From that moment his life radically changed. He quit his job because he said it didn't honor God. He had been smoking three packs of cigarettes a day; he immediately quit. He started sharing the Gospel with everyone he met. My mom and both sides of the family believed he had lost his mind, so they went before a judge to have him committed to a mental institution. Everyone signed the papers, but at the very last minute my mom could not do it and he was not committed. But they agreed to part ways.

After all this, my mom was confused and seeking answers. She went first to her father and asked to speak to the rabbi. He told her, "You've brought enough shame on our family already. You may not speak to him." She went to another religious leader, but he required twenty-five dollars. She was desperate and alone. With nowhere else to go, she checked into a hotel and it was there she found a Bible, tucked away in a drawer. She then began praying, and God heard her cries and responded.

Her Bible opened to Psalm 116:

"I love the LORD, for he heard my voice;
he heard my cry for mercy.
Because he turned his ear to me,
I will call on him as long as I live.

The cords of death entangled me,
the anguish of the grave came over me;
I was overcome by distress and sorrow.
Then I called on the name of the LORD:
'LORD save me!'

…When I was brought low, he saved me….

For you, LORD, have delivered me from death,
my eyes from tears,
and my feet from stumbling." (1–4, 6, 8)

That night she received Jesus as her Messiah, her Savior and Lord. She called my dad and said she wanted to return home. "How are you coming?" he inquired. "Saved!" was her joyful reply.

Shortly thereafter, they felt God's call into full-time ministry and headed to Bible school. But many challenges lay ahead. When Aileen went to her parents to share her decision for Christ, her mother tried to kill her. She told Mom, "I'd rather have you dead than believe in Jesus

Christ!" The police came. My grandfather suffered a heart attack. It would be many years before they would see each other again, and years before the hurt and pain was replaced with love and acceptance.

When I was around six years of age, my parents decided to move to Columbus, Ohio. They began a ministry called The Conversion Center. My father had a small house church and worked as a tailor to support our growing family. My grandparents wanted to see us, and they reached out. God had softened their hearts and used them to help support us financially. It was the beginning of restoring what had been broken.

We began to see them on a regular basis, and how we loved them! Grandpa was loving, generous, and kind. My parents would share Jesus with them each time we met. My grandfather would respond, "If only I had been told when I was young. Now I'm too old." We were overjoyed to know he made a decision for Christ on his deathbed. My grandmother also accepted Jesus as her Messiah after my grandfather's death.

God's love restored what was broken. He brought life from death; light from darkness.

The names of God beautifully reflect His character and power. As I retell my mom's story, those names bear special significance to me.

Jehovah-Rohi, *the Lord my Shepherd*, restores our souls.

Jehovah-Shalom, *the Lord who is peace*, brings calm in the midst of life's storms.

Jehovah-Nissi, *the Lord is my banner*, shields us and gives us victory.

Jehovah-Jireh, *the Lord who provides*, supplies our needs.

Jehovah-Rapha, *the Lord is my healer*, mends our physical and emotional wounds.

All of this can take place because He is Jehovah-Tsidkenu, *the Lord our righteousness*, who has made us righteous by His own blood.

QUESTIONS

1. Which name of God has special significance in your life and why?

....

....

2. Name two ways God's love was shown in Aileen's story.

....

....

....

3. Is God's love dependent upon anything we do?

....

....

....

....

DAY 2

A PSALM

REFLECTION

Psalm 116 was my mother's favorite psalm. I heard her share it so many times, as a girl I committed it to memory. As I shared in yesterday's study, within the pages of a Bible, she discovered this psalm. Immediately the scales were removed from her eyes and that very night she received Jesus into her heart and became His daughter forever. My mother understood early on the cost of discipleship, the cost of following Jesus. But for her it wasn't a sacrifice. She was in love with Jesus.

PSALM 116

I love the LORD, for he heard my voice;
he heard my cry for mercy.
Because he turned his ear to me,
I will call on him as long as I live.

The cords of death entangled me,
the anguish of the grave came over me;
I was overcome by distress and sorrow.
Then I called on the name of the LORD:
"LORD, save me!"

The LORD is gracious and righteous;
our God is full of compassion.
The LORD protects the unwary;
when I was brought low, he saved me.

Return to your rest, my soul,
for the LORD has been good to you.

For you, LORD, have delivered me from death,
my eyes from tears,
my feet from stumbling,
that I may walk before the LORD
in the land of the living.

I trusted in the LORD when I said,
"I am greatly afflicted";
in my alarm I said,
"Everyone is a liar."

What shall I return to the LORD
for all his goodness to me?

I will lift up the cup of salvation
and call on the name of the LORD.
I will fulfill my vows to the LORD
in the presence of all his people.

Precious in the sight of the Lord
is the death of his faithful servants.
Truly I am your servant, Lord;
I serve you just as my mother did;
you have freed me from my chains.
I will sacrifice a thank offering to you
and call on the name of the Lord.
I will fulfill my vows to the Lord
in the presence of all his people,
in the courts of the house of the Lord—
in your midst, Jerusalem.

Praise the Lord.

In the psalm above, highlight in RED what speaks to your heart.
Highlight in YELLOW what God might be inviting you to do.
Highlight in BLUE God's promises.

Hymn of Praise

REFLECTION

"My Jesus, I Love Thee" is a song of adoration to the One who loves us sacrificially and unconditionally. Whether you choose to read and meditate on the words, sing along with a recording, or worshipfully dance to the music, let it be your love song to Jesus.

MY JESUS, I LOVE THEE
1864, William R. Featherson

My Jesus, I love Thee; I know Thou art mine;
For Thee all the follies of sin I resign;
My gracious Redeemer, My Savior art Thou;
If ever I loved Thee, my Jesus, 'tis now.

I love Thee because Thou hast first loved me,
And purchased my pardon on Calvary's tree;
I love Thee for wearing the thorns on Thy brow;
If ever I loved Thee, my Jesus, 'tis now.

In mansions of glory and endless delight,
I'll ever adore Thee in heaven so bright;
I'll sing with the glittering crown on my brow,
If ever I loved Thee, my Jesus, 'tis now.

DAY 4

Digging Deeper

STUDY

The ultimate example of sacrificial and unconditional love is the sinless Jesus dying in our place, saving us from our sins. Our Creator, the God of the universe, sacrificed His one and only Son on our behalf. John 3:16, which reads, "For God so loved the world that he gave his one and only Son, that whoever believes in him shall not perish but have eternal life," is said to be one of the most read verses in the entire Bible. It is a compelling invitation for the world to know and understand the depth of God's love for each one of us, and a simple invitation to receive His love and be assured of eternal life with God the Father, God the Son, and God the Holy Spirit forever. It requires us to simply believe; believe in the One who sent Jesus and believe in Jesus himself so that we might be saved. "If you declare with your mouth, 'Jesus is Lord,' and believe in your heart that God raised him from the dead, you will be saved" (Romans 10:9).

"They replied, 'Believe in the Lord Jesus, and you will be saved'" (Acts 16:31). Rich or poor, young or old, this invitation is open to every man, woman and child in the entire world. That's how much God loves you and desires you to be part of His forever family.

As a little girl, I remember a plaque that hung in our kitchen with 1 John 3:18 inscribed on it: "Dear children, let us not love with words or speech but with actions and in truth." It served as a daily reminder to live and walk in love.

We have been called to love. The Greatest Commandment declares that we are to love God with all our heart, soul, mind, and strength, and love others as ourselves (see Matthew 22:37–39). Our priority is to love; love God and love people.

But Jesus went further when He instructed that we are to love our enemies. "I tell you, love your enemies and pray for those who persecute you, that you may be children of your Father in heaven" (Matthew 5:44–45).

We are not only commanded to love our enemies and pray for them but do good to them. I don't know about you, but in my own strength this would be inconceivable. Jesus continues with laser-beam focus and exhorts that there is nothing special about loving those who love us. Even the world does that. In other words, Jesus raises the bar to His standard of love and demands we do the seemingly impossible: love your enemies, do good to them, and expect nothing in return. Then what does He say? "Your reward will be great, and you will be children of the Most High" (Luke 6:35). Jesus is challenging us to love exactly as He loved when He walked this earth. If we are indeed His children, we will love the way He loves— the way He commands us to love.

"But to you who are listening I say: Love your enemies, do good to those who hate you, bless those who curse you, pray for those who mistreat you" (Luke 6:27–28).

"If you love those who love you, what credit is that to you? Even sinners love those who love them. And if you do good to those who are good to you, what credit is that to you? Even sinners do that. And if you lend to those from whom you expect repayment, what credit is that to you? Even sinners lend to sinners, expecting to be repaid in full. But love your enemies, do good to them, and lend to them without expecting to get anything back. Then your reward will be great, and you will be children of the Most High, because he is kind to the ungrateful and wicked. Be merciful, just as your Father is merciful" (Luke 6:32–36).

"To this you were called, because Christ suffered for you, leaving you an example, that you should follow in his steps" (1 Peter 2:21).

From the agony of the cross Jesus cried, "Father, forgive them, for they do not know what they are doing" (Luke 23:34). Jesus prayed for those who tortured Him. It is impossible for us to love like Jesus, forgive like Jesus, and serve like Jesus without His love, His forgiveness, and His servant heart flowing through us.

But what might happen if you intentionally pray and

ask God, "Help me love You with my whole heart. Help me love others the way You love me."

Jesus makes it clear. When we abide in Christ and His words abide in us, our Christ-centered prayers will be answered.

"If you remain in me and my words remain in you, ask whatever you wish, and it will be done for you" (John 15:7).

"[We] receive from him anything we ask, because we keep his commands and do what pleases him" (1 John 3:22).

"This is the confidence we have in approaching God: that if we ask anything according to his will, he hears us" (1 John 5:14).

"I will do whatever you ask in my name, so that the Father may be glorified in the Son. You may ask me for anything in my name, and I will do it" (John 14:13–14).

I've experienced His answers many times in my own life, and am convinced that He will answer your prayers and answer them quickly when you are praying for His perfect will to be done. It is the will of God that you love Him more than anything in the entire world, including your spouse, children, parents, friends, and enemies. For when you love Jesus above all things, you will love your spouse, children, parents, friends, and enemies well, because He will love through you with the same grace, forgiveness, and goodness with which He loves you.

In her book *No Greater Love*, Mother Teresa writes about how to love Jesus:

> "Love Jesus generously. Love Him trustfully, without looking back and without fear. Give yourself fully to Jesus. He will use you to accomplish great things on the condition that you believe much more in His love than in your weakness. Believe in Him, trust in Him with a blind and absolute confidence because He is Jesus."

REFLECTION

There are so many verses on love in the Bible. Here are just a few more to serve as gentle reminders of the necessity of love and how we have been called to love.

> Above all, love each other deeply, because love covers over a multitude of sins. (1 Peter 4:8)

> A new command I give you: Love one another. As I have loved you, so you must love one another. By this everyone will know that you are my disciples, if you love one another. (John 13:34–35)

Do everything in love. (1 Corinthians 16:14)

If you love me, keep my commands. (John 14:15)

Jesus replied, "Anyone who loves me will obey my teaching. My Father will love them, and we will come to them and make our home with them." (John 14:23)

QUESTIONS

1. What does love mean to you?

....

....

2. List one example of how and when you have experienced love.

....

....

3. What is the most challenging aspect of love for you?

....

....

4. What makes God's love so amazing to you personally?

....

....

PRAYER

Dear Heavenly Father, how great is the love You have lavished on us, that we should be called Your children! Thank You for Your grace that has made me Your dearly loved daughter. Help me love You with my whole heart. Help me love others as You love me, sacrificially and unconditionally. Help me love my enemies, Father; I cannot do this without You. I ask that You love through me all those who have hurt or offended me. I ask now that You create in me a clean heart, O God, and renew a right spirit within me. Father, forgive me when I do not love You as I should. Help me to love like You do, Jesus, and keep Your commandments. Make me a channel of Your love and grace to every person in my life so that You may be glorified in me. Love through me, bless through me, forgive through me.

I ask all this in Your precious and holy name. Amen.

ACTION STEPS

1. What makes love so appealing to you?

....

....

....

....

....

2. How will you apply this in your daily life?

....

....

....

....

....

3. With whom will you share this truth?

....

....

....

....

....

....

....

CHAPTER 3

COMPASSION
Homeless and Alone

MEMORY VERSE

My command is this:
Love each other as I have loved you.

JOHN 15:12

DAY 1

Definition of Compassion

A sympathetic consciousness of others' distress together
with a desire to alleviate it

PRAYER

Dear Heavenly Father,
Thank You for loving me and making me Your daughter.
Help me love You with my whole heart.
Help me love others the way You love me.
Thank You for washing away my sins and making me clean.
Help me rejoice in You always, in spite of my circumstances.
I want to follow You as my Lord and Savior.
Fill me with Your Holy Spirit. Make me a woman after
Your own heart.
Make me an instrument of Your grace, truth, and justice.
Use me for Your glory and to be a blessing to others.
Gracious Father, I pray in the name of Jesus Christ our
Savior and in the power of the Holy Spirit. Amen.

STUDY

As you begin this study, carefully read the definition of
compassion, pray the prayer, and review your memory verse.

I was deeply moved reading this testimony of a
graduate student at the Ohio State University School
of Social Work. She has a special place in her heart for

45

veterans, desiring to improve their lives. This is her account of what occurred on Christmas Eve, 2019.

ALLY'S STORY

> This is how we know what love is: Jesus Christ laid down his life for us. And we ought to lay down our lives for our brothers and sisters. If anyone has material possessions and sees a brother or sister in need but has no pity on them, how can the love of God be in that person? Dear children, let us not love with words or speech but with actions and in truth. (1 John 3:16–18)

It was Christmas Eve, and on my way home from the post office I passed the grocery store. There was a homeless man standing outside by the parking lot entrance, holding a sign. I had seen him several times over the summer and fall but had never spoken to him. As soon as I passed him, my heart was telling me, "Go back and help him." I thought, *No, I'm cold and tired. I just want to go home.* So, I continued on my drive home. As I entered my neighborhood the feeling became very strong, and I turned around and went back to where I had seen him. I prayed as I walked toward him and was confident that God would give me the words to say.

I asked, "Are you hungry?" He replied, "Yes ma'am, I am." He had a cane and some bags with him. I offered to carry his bags into the store as we went to get something to eat. "I have to carry my bags now, or managers will know I'm homeless and think I'm begging. They've threatened to kick me out before." I told him that as long as he was with me, he'd be fine.

We went to the deli and got a hot piece of chicken. That's all he wanted. "You can get more, it's okay," I said. "Get some extra as leftovers." He then started to tell me he was a plumber in the navy and served on an aircraft carrier and had been called to the first Gulf War. He got injured in the navy and had to medically retire. He gets some disability money, but not enough to live on. To make matters worse, his wife got sick right before Thanksgiving. Doctors told her she would die if she left the hospital. A few days after leaving the hospital, she died.

He went on, "I give almost half of my disability money to my sister, who is taking care of my ten-year-old daughter in Dayton." He showed me some pictures of a beautiful, young red-headed girl. He talked about everything she wanted for Christmas, and he used his disability money to buy things for her. "I only get to see her about once every month, and I miss her."

He asked me to look up how much a Greyhound bus ticket would cost for the next day, which was Christmas. "If you leave early enough, they're only seven dollars," I said. "That's good, I can scrape some money together to get a ticket and see her." I grabbed a Visa gift card and said, "Guess what? You're going to see your daughter tomorrow." He immediately burst into tears and thanked me profusely.

"Everyone deserves to see their kids on Christmas. You're a good dad and you deserve to see her." He excitedly told me he would use the extra money to bring her some Christmas presents. As we walked outside so he could finish eating his lunch, we continued our conversation.

"What's your name?"

"Ally," I responded. He looked at me with huge eyes and said, "That's my daughter's name, Allison Marie." I knew right then why God had told me to go back. He gave me a hug and thanked me again.

As I walked back to my car, I knew this Christmas memory was one that would stay with me forever.

Ally was tired, it was cold, and she was ready to relax for the night. It would have been so easy to brush off the encounter, but she was sensitive to the leading of the Holy Spirit so instead of putting herself first, Ally put this homeless man ahead of her desires, her needs, and her wants. She saw him through the eyes of Jesus, and she showed compassion. In a world of me-first, nonstop hustle and bustle, it takes an intentional desire to love others like Jesus. It won't happen in our own strength; it will happen only when we open our hearts to His and follow in His steps.

QUESTIONS

1. What emotions stirred within you as you read Ally's story?

....

....

....

2. What stood out to you the most?

....

....

....

3. How do you think you would have reacted in the same situation?

....

....

....

4. How can you be more intentional in showing compassion to others in need?

....

....

....

....

....

A Psalm

REFLECTION

Did you know you are crowned with the Father's love and compassion? He blesses you with good things, He heals your diseases, and forgives your sin. He strengthens you and lifts you up on eagle's wings. Psalm 103 is a beautiful invitation to receive the Lord's blessing as His precious daughters, and as His daughters to bless Him, honor Him, and thank Him for His loving kindness, His goodness, and the mercy that He daily bestows on us.

The 103rd Psalm is a beautiful love song reflecting God's character that you can sing or pray. It will amaze, delight, and comfort you each time it is read.

PSALM 103
A Psalm of David

Praise the LORD, my soul;
all my inmost being, praise his holy name.
Praise the LORD, my soul,
and forget not all his benefits—
who forgives all your sins
and heals all your diseases,
who redeems your life from the pit

and crowns you with love and compassion,
who satisfies your desires with good things
so that your youth is renewed like the eagle's.

The LORD works righteousness
and justice for all the oppressed.

He made known his ways to Moses,
his deeds to the people of Israel:
The LORD is compassionate and gracious,
slow to anger, abounding in love.
He will not always accuse,
nor will he harbor his anger forever;
he does not treat us as our sins deserve
or repay us according to our iniquities.
For as high as the heavens are above the earth,
so great is his love for those who fear him;
as far as the east is from the west,
so far has he removed our transgressions from us.

As a father has compassion on his children,
so the LORD has compassion on those who fear him;
for he knows how we are formed,
he remembers that we are dust.
The life of mortals is like grass,
they flourish like a flower of the field;
the wind blows over it and it is gone,
and its place remembers it no more.

But from everlasting to everlasting
the LORD's love is with those who fear him,
and his righteousness with their children's children—
with those who keep his covenant
and remember to obey his precepts.

The LORD has established his throne in heaven,
and his kingdom rules over all.

Praise the LORD, you his angels,
you mighty ones who do his bidding,
who obey his word.
Praise the LORD, all his heavenly hosts,
you his servants who do his will.
Praise the LORD, all his works
everywhere in his dominion.

Praise the LORD, O my soul.

In the psalm above, highlight in RED what speaks to your heart.
Highlight in YELLOW what God might be inviting you to do.
Highlight in BLUE God's promises.

Hymn of Praise

REFLECTION

This great hymn of the faith was written by Thomas Chisholm in 1923. Thomas wrote 1,200 hymns during his lifetime. One of his favorite scriptures was Lamentations 3:22–23: "His compassions never fail. They are new every morning; great is your faithfulness." Inspired by these verses, he wrote this beloved and well-known hymn.

Whether you choose to read and meditate on the words, sing along with a recording, or worshipfully dance to the music, may your heart be stirred, and your soul filled.

GREAT IS THY FAITHFULNESS

1923, by Thomas Chisholm

Great is Thy faithfulness, O God my Father,
There is no shadow of turning with Thee;
Thou changest not, Thy compassions, they fail not.
As Thou hast been Thou forever wilt be.

Summer and winter, and springtime and harvest,
Sun, moon, and stars in their courses above,

Join with all nature in manifold witness
To Thy great faithfulness, mercy, and love.

Pardon for sin and a peace that endureth,
Thine own dear presence to cheer and to guide;
Strength for today and bright hope for tomorrow,
Blessings all mine, with ten thousand beside!

Great is Thy faithfulness, Great is Thy faithfulness,
Morning by morning new mercies I see.
All I have needed Thy hand hath provided.
Great is Thy faithfulness, Lord, unto me.

DAY 4

Digging Deeper

STUDY

Jesus was often moved with compassion. He taught about it and demonstrated it throughout His ministry on earth. One stunning example is found in John 8:3–11.

> The teachers of the law and the Pharisees brought in a woman caught in adultery. They made her stand before the group and said to Jesus, "Teacher, this woman was caught in the act of adultery. In the Law Moses commanded us to stone such women. Now what do you say?" They were using this question as a trap, in order to have a basis for accusing him.
>
> But Jesus bent down and started to write on the ground with his finger. When they kept on questioning him, he straightened up and said to them, "Let any one of you who is without sin be the first to throw a stone at her." Again he stooped down and wrote on the ground.
>
> At this, those who heard began to go away one at a time, the older ones first, until only Jesus was left, with the woman still standing there. Jesus straightened up and asked her, "Woman, where are they? Has no one condemned you?"

"No one, sir," she said.

"Then neither do I condemn you," Jesus declared. "Go now and leave your life of sin."

Even today, in certain cultures, women caught in adultery are being stoned to death. The religious leaders in Jesus' time were passing judgment on a woman who was guilty of having an affair. Notice the words "they made her stand before the group" as they brought her to Jesus. I can't begin to imagine her shame and embarrassment as they forced her to stand publicly before a crowd who was condemning her to death.

Jesus was silent and simply bent down and began writing in the dirt with His finger. What was He writing? These leaders humiliated this woman publicly and announced her sin before the crowd. The Bible does not say what Jesus wrote in the sand, but what if He was writing the sins of those standing to watch, eagerly awaiting her punishment?

"Let any one of you who is without sin be the first to throw a stone at her."

He continued writing on the ground… Lying? Adultery? Covetousness? Pride? Jealousy? These evil deeds were visible to the One who sees everything, because He knows the heart (Acts 15:8); Jesus highlighted the accusers' sin until, one by one, they began to walk away. And notice, the older ones left first, recognizing their life of sin they thought was safely hidden from sight in fact made them worthy of a similar fate.

I love the way Jesus always asked poignant questions: "Woman, where are they? Has no one condemned you?"

Can you imagine how she felt? This Man she'd never met, but no doubt had heard about, became her advocate and defender. He shielded and freed her from her accusers and an agonizing death sentence. With a heart full of compassion, He released and forgave her: "Neither do I condemn you. Go now and leave your life of sin."

Jesus has done that for you and me. Because of His grace, love, and compassion, He freed us from death and from our deserved punishment.

> "Therefore, there is now no condemnation for those who are in Christ Jesus, because through Christ Jesus the law of the Spirit who gives life has set you free from the law of sin and death" (Romans 8:1–2).

> "Therefore, as God's chosen people, holy and dearly loved, clothe yourselves with compassion, kindness, humility, gentleness and patience" (Colossians 3:12).

QUESTIONS

1. Write a list of your sins on a piece of paper. Tear up the sheet of paper and throw it away.

2. Write out Romans 8:1.

....

....

....

....

....

3. Remember the words of Jesus in Matthew 7:1–2: "Do not judge, or you too will be judged. For in the same way you judge others, you will be judged, and with the measure you use, it will be measured to you."

....

....

....

4. Is there someone you have judged or condemned wrongly? Ask Jesus to forgive you and seek their forgiveness.

....

....

....

PRAYER

Dear Heavenly Father, thank You for being loving, gracious, rich in mercy, and full of compassion. Thank You for not giving me what I deserve. Thank You that there is no condemnation toward those who belong to You. Thank You for being my Advocate and Defender, for crowning me with Your love and compassion, and for satisfying me with good things. Father, give me Your heart for those around me. Break my heart for what breaks Yours. Help me not to judge others but show Your loving-kindness in all that I do and say. Make me more like You, Jesus.

In Your holy name I pray. Amen.

ACTION STEPS

1. What makes compassion so appealing to you?

....
....
....
....
....

2. How will you apply this in your daily life?

....
....
....
....
....

3. With whom will you share this truth?

....
....
....
....
....
....
....
....

CHAPTER 4

REPENTANCE
Freedom in Forgiveness

MEMORY VERSE

Have mercy on me, O God,
according to your unfailing love;
according to your great compassion
blot out my transgressions.
Wash away all my iniquity
and cleanse me from my sin.

PSALM 51:1–2

DAY 1

Definition of Repentance

The action or process of repenting,
especially for misdeeds or moral shortcomings

PRAYER

Dear Heavenly Father,
Thank You for loving me and making me Your daughter.
Help me love You with my whole heart.
Help me love others the way You love me.
Thank You for washing away my sins and making me clean.
Help me rejoice in You always, in spite of my circumstances.
I want to follow You as my Lord and Savior.
Fill me with Your Holy Spirit. Make me a woman after
     Your own heart.
Make me an instrument of Your grace, truth, and justice.
Use me for Your glory and to be a blessing to others.
Gracious Father, I pray in the name of Jesus Christ our
     Savior and in the power of the Holy Spirit. Amen.

STUDY

As you begin the study, carefully read the definition of
repentance, pray the prayer, and review your memory verse.

Holy, holy, holy is the Lord God Almighty, who was,
and is, and is to come. (Revelation 4:8)

But just as he who called you is holy, so be holy in all you do; for it is written: "Be holy, because I am holy." (1 Peter 1:15–16)

Christ has called us to holiness because He is holy. He encompasses all that is holy and pure. For this reason, we must daily repent of our sins—anything that separates us from Christ. If there is unconfessed sin, if we are harboring any ill feelings toward another or unforgiveness within our hearts, our prayers will not reach heaven.

Repentance and forgiveness are integrally linked. Oftentimes Christians need to repent of the spirit of unforgiveness. It is dangerous, kept deep within us, hidden from public view. The effects of an unforgiving spirit wreak havoc on our physical bodies as well as our spiritual and emotional well-being. Pastors, attorneys, and medical workers all have seen the ravaging effects bitterness has on the body, mind, and soul. It is no wonder that Jesus talked about it so often and warned of its severe consequences.

We recognize as a society that stealing, murder, kidnapping, and adultery are evil and sinful acts. It is easy to look upon the sins of David lusting after Bathsheba, committing adultery, and murdering her husband so they could marry, and recognize the wickedness of his deeds. It should not surprise us that God sent the prophet Nathan to convict him of his sin.

But what about the sin of gossip? Is that not also a sin that will separate us from God's holiness? What about the sin of an unforgiving spirit? Sometimes we harbor hurt feelings over the smallest, most trivial act committed toward us. We feed on it, allow Satan to stir up resentment within us, and instead of releasing it to Jesus and asking for His help, we hide it deep inside or share it with others, which makes it even worse. And then we wonder why our prayers go unanswered and we lack joy and peace. And what about unforgiveness in your heart that seems justifiable because of an egregious action of another towards you? Can that become sin?

In *Reflections of God's Glory*, Corrie ten Boom shares a powerful story about forgiveness when, after speaking at a church in Munich, a former SS officer who had guarded her in the concentration camp began walking toward her. He wanted to shake her hand, but the pain and suffering he had caused her made it seemingly impossible. Thank God He knows our hearts. He knew what Corrie was battling within, and as she stretched out her hand to receive his, the anger and pain dissipated to joy, and the overwhelming knowledge that the Holy Spirit stepped in and miraculously forgave through her.

Only Jesus, by the power of His Holy Spirit, can help us do the seemingly impossible. We need only a willing heart. Corrie wrote, "When He tells us to love our enemies, He gives, along with the command, the love itself."

QUESTIONS

1. What is the difference between repentance and forgiveness?

....

....

....

....

2. Which is more difficult and why?

....

....

....

....

3. How do you think Corrie ten Boom must have felt facing the man who caused her so much pain and humiliation?

....

....

....

....

....

....

....

....

DAY 2

A PSALM

REFLECTION

Psalm 51 is a wonderful way to begin your prayer time each day. It is David's prayer of repentance for the sin committed with Bathsheba after being confronted by the prophet Nathan. It is a prayer of renewal and restoration, as God makes all things new when we simply ask.

PSALM 51

Have mercy on me, O God,
according to your unfailing love;
according to your great compassion
blot out my transgressions.
Wash away all my iniquity
and cleanse me from my sin.

For I know my transgressions,
and my sin is always before me.
Against you, you only, have I sinned
and done what is evil in your sight;
so you are right in your verdict
and justified when you judge.
Surely I was sinful at birth,
sinful from the time my mother conceived me.

Yet you desired faithfulness even in the womb;
you taught me wisdom in that secret place.

Cleanse me with hyssop, and I will be clean;
wash me, and I will be whiter than snow.
Let me hear joy and gladness;
let the bones you have crushed rejoice.
Hide your face from my sins
and blot out all my iniquity.

Create in me a pure heart, O God,
and renew a steadfast spirit within me.
Do not cast me from your presence
or take your Holy Spirit from me.
Restore to me the joy of your salvation
and grant me a willing spirit, to sustain me.

Then I will teach transgressors your ways,
so that sinners will turn back to you.
Deliver me from the guilt of bloodshed, O God,
you who are God my Savior,
and my tongue will sing of your righteousness.
Open my lips, Lord,
and my mouth will declare your praise.
You do not delight in sacrifice, or I would bring it;
you do not take pleasure in burnt offerings.
My sacrifice, O God, is a broken spirit;

a broken and contrite heart
you, God, will not despise.

May it please you to prosper Zion,
to build up the walls of Jerusalem.
Then you will delight in the sacrifices of the righteous,
in burnt offerings offered whole;
then bulls will be offered on your altar.

In the psalm above, highlight in RED what speaks to your heart.
Highlight in YELLOW what God might be inviting you to do.
Highlight in BLUE God's promises.

Hymn of Praise

REFLECTION

The great hymn that many have come to know and love from the Billy Graham Crusades is "Just As I Am." It was written in 1836 by Charlotte Elliott. Her poor health had hardened her heart and made her bitter toward God. She blamed Him for her ailments. In May 1822, a pastor visited their home. At dinner, Charlotte lost her temper and her anger toward God and her family poured out. The pastor lovingly shared that she was clinging to her hate and anger because she had nothing else to cling to and offered her the hope that only Jesus could bring. He challenged her to give herself to Jesus—all of her anger, fear, and shame. When she said she didn't know how, the pastor's encouraging words, "You have only to come to Him just as you are," became the inspiration for the song. She claimed John 6:37, "Whoever comes to me I will never drive away." She authored approximately 150 hymns in her lifetime.

JUST AS I AM
1836, by Charlotte Elliott

Just as I am without one plea,
But that Thy blood was shed for me,
And that Thou bidst me come to Thee,
O Lamb of God, I come. I come.

Just as I am and waiting not
To rid my soul of one dark blot,
To Thee whose blood can cleanse each spot,
O Lamb of God, I come. I come.

Just as I am, though tossed about
With many a conflict, many a doubt,
Fightings and fears within, without,
O Lamb of God, I come, I come.

Just as I am, Thou wilt receive,
Wilt welcome, pardon, cleanse, relieve.
Because Thy promise I believe,
O Lamb of God, I come, I come.

Whether you choose to read and meditate on the words, sing along with a recording, or worshipfully dance to the music, may your heart be stirred, and your soul filled.

Digging Deeper

STUDY

Remember our first lesson, on grace—something we didn't earn and something we don't deserve. Are we able to extend God's grace and forgive those who have wronged us? Are we able to love God enough to forgive those who have hurt us, just as He commanded? Are we able to release pent-up anger or grudges against them? Can we forgive like Jesus forgives?

In Matthew 6:15 Jesus shares these sobering words, "But if you do not forgive others their sins, your Father will not forgive your sins." C. S. Lewis, in his book *Mere Christianity*, wrote about what he believed to be the most unpopular Christian rule, "Thou shalt love thy neighbor as thyself." He went on to explain, "Because in Christian morals 'thy neighbor' includes 'thy enemy,' and so we come up against this terrible duty of forgiving our enemies.… Everyone says forgiveness is a lovely idea, until they have something to forgive."

Forgiveness is often a litmus test God uses before releasing men and women into all kinds of ministry. This is such an important principle and ties into all our themes thus far. The act of forgiveness involves grace, love, compassion, and repentance. The themes for the daily prayer are interwoven, as you will find when we continue on to commitment, dependence (Holy Spirit), influence, discipleship, and authority. Grace is foundational for forgiveness. Because of God's limitless grace, boundless love, and compassion, He extends His forgiveness to us. But that is only the beginning. When we recognize the magnitude of our own sin and selfishness, when we see how we fall short in the presence of a perfect, holy, and pure Savior, how can we be unwilling to forgive someone who has sinned against us? To love as God does, we must also be willing to extend His forgiveness to others.

Think of the story of the unforgiving servant in Matthew 18:21–35. The King forgives a debt so huge, his servant would not have been able to repay it over his entire lifetime. This servant begged for mercy and experienced the love, grace, compassion, and forgiveness of a benevolent king. Yet when it was his turn to offer that same forgiveness to someone who owed him only a tiny sum, his heart grew cold and he refused. Instead, he threw him into prison, ignoring his cries for mercy. When the King found out what he had done, his anger was kindled, and he gave him the punishment he so deserved. Thus, Jesus' warning, "If you do not forgive others their sins, your Father will not forgive your sins."

Our family went through a terribly painful and traumatic experience with a family member. It split our extended family apart. During that time, I remember hearing a sermon on forgiveness: "Begin praying for the person who wronged you. If you can only pray, 'God bless so and so,' then begin with those few words." Though it was not easy, I did it. Immediately following my prayer came a heavenly outpouring of compassion and grief for the person who committed the offense. It was as if Jesus was waiting for me to take that initial step, to show a willing heart, then He supernaturally stepped in and the Spirit of God did the rest.

The older I get, the more I realize how unworthy I am to be a child of God. I relate to Paul's words in 1 Timothy 1:15, "Christ Jesus came into the world to save sinners—of whom I am the worst." Isaiah wrote, "All our righteous acts are like filthy rags" (64:6). How precious the reassuring words found in Titus 3:4–5: "But when the kindness and love of God our Savior appeared, he saved us, not because of righteous things we had done, but because of his mercy."

QUESTIONS

1. List one example of when you experienced forgiveness.

....

....

....

2. List one example of when you forgave someone and extended mercy.

....

....

....

3. Share a verse on forgiveness that speaks to your heart.

....

....

....

....

4. Is there someone you need to forgive? Do it today, without delay!

....

....

....

....

....

DAY 5

PRAYER

Dear Heavenly Father, we recognize You are a holy God, and from Your throne flow truth and righteousness. We know we are unworthy to be called Your children apart from Your love, grace, and mercy. Thank You that the blood of Your Son, Jesus, cleanses me from all sin. I ask that You create in me a clean heart and renew a right spirit within me. Lead me in the way everlasting. Transform me day by day into the image of Your Son. Show me if there is any sin in my life and help me repent and turn away from all that separates me from Your love. Heal broken relationships and remove any bitterness. Help me to always forgive others the way You have forgiven me, enabling me to walk in newness of life and experience the joy of being Your daughter.

In Jesus' name I pray. Amen.

ACTION STEPS

1. What makes repentance and forgiveness so appealing to you?

....
....
....
....
....

2. How will you apply this in your daily life?

....
....
....
....
....

3. With whom will you share this truth?

....
....
....
....
....
....
....

....
....
....
....
....
....
....
....
....
....
....
....
....
....
....
....
....
....
....
....
....
....
....
....

CHAPTER 5

WORSHIP
Mary's Magnificat

MEMORY VERSE

Let everything that has breath
praise the LORD.

PSALM 150:6

DAY 1

Definition of Worship

Extravagant respect or admiration for or devotion
to an object of esteem

PRAYER

Dear Heavenly Father,
Thank You for loving me and making me Your daughter.
Help me love You with my whole heart.
Help me love others the way You love me.
Thank You for washing away my sins and making me clean.
Help me rejoice in You always, in spite of my circumstances.
I want to follow You as my Lord and Savior.
Fill me with Your Holy Spirit. Make me a woman after Your
*   own heart.*
Make me an instrument of Your grace, truth, and justice.
Use me for Your glory and to be a blessing to others.
Gracious Father, I pray in the name of Jesus Christ our
*   Savior and in the power of the Holy Spirit. Amen.*

STUDY

As you begin the study, carefully read the definition of
worship, pray the daily prayer, and review your memory
verse.

When I think of worship, what immediately comes to
mind is the prayer of Mary found in Luke 1:46–55. After

Gabriel's visit announcing to Mary that she would be with child, carrying the One conceived by the Holy Spirit, the Messiah, she immediately packed her things and went to visit her relative Elizabeth.

Elizabeth and her husband, Zechariah, also had been visited by Gabriel and received surprising news. In their old age, Elizabeth would conceive and bear the greatest prophet, John the Baptist, the forerunner of Jesus the Messiah.

Two women, two miracles, two divine appointments by an angel, and two unborn men—one who would announce the coming of the Lamb of God, and One who was the Lamb.

Mary, a young, unmarried girl, engaged to Joseph and pregnant by the power of the Most High, and Elizabeth, an old woman who was barren, now pregnant with Zechariah's baby because of God's supernatural intervention, marvel at God's goodness in their lives.

I can only imagine what was going through Mary's mind when she found out she would carry God's Son inside of her. She was filled with great faith even at such a young age, even though there would certainly be many difficulties ahead. I love Gabriel's word to her in Luke 1:37: "No word from God will ever fail." If we only believed that with all our hearts, how might God use us? Mary's response to Gabriel was that of faith and humility. "'I am the Lord's servant,' Mary answered. 'May your word to me be fulfilled'" (1:38).

It is significant to note how Elizabeth received Mary. Upon greeting her, she offered a beautiful blessing:

"Blessed are you among women, and blessed is the child you will bear! But why am I so favored, that the mother of my Lord should come to me?…Blessed is she who has believed that the Lord would fulfill his promises to her!" (Luke 1:42–43, 45)

Mary must have been frightened and unsure about all that was happening to her and perhaps seeking reassurance from someone older and wiser. I imagine she rejoiced in hearing Elizabeth's words of blessing. Note that verse 41 says that Elizabeth was filled with the Holy Spirit. Her humility was evident in recognizing that Mary's child was even more important than the one she carried within her. There was no jealousy or tension; only love, joy, and affirmation.

Then comes Mary's exquisite song, or Magnificat:

"My soul glorifies the Lord
and my spirit rejoices in God my Savior,
for he has been mindful
of the humble state of his servant.
From now on all generations will call me blessed,
for the Mighty One has done great things for me—
holy is his name.

His mercy extends to those who fear him,
from generation to generation.
He has performed mighty deeds with his arm;
he has scattered those who are proud in their inmost
thoughts.
He has brought down rulers from their thrones
but has lifted up the humble.
He has filled the hungry with good things
but has sent the rich away empty.
He has helped his servant Israel,
remembering to be merciful
to Abraham and his descendants forever,
just as he promised our ancestors."

Do we believe God's promises? He has given us His Word to speak to us; He has given us His Holy Spirit to guide and teach us. Are we listening? Are we trusting Him for all He has promised? Are we spending time with Him each day? Are we becoming more like Him?

QUESTIONS

1. What stands out to you in Mary's song?

....

....

....

....

2. Has God ever stirred within you in such a way that you have burst into a song or a prayer? If so, write it in the lines below.

....

....

....

....

....

3. Write your own worship poem or your favorite worship verse below.

....

....

....

....

....

....

....

A Psalm

REFLECTION

As a girl growing up, there was a pastor in my life who always responded to every "How are you?" that came his way with a resounding, "Praising the Lord!" That is not always easy to do. In the midst of stressful circumstances, packed schedules, financial worries, family crises, and the like, we often forget that God is still in control. He is forever faithful, omnipotent, omniscient, omnipresent, the God of time and eternity.

How can we learn to praise Him in the midst of difficulty? How do we extend a heart of praise past the Sunday morning worship time? How do we grow in the knowledge that we were created by Him and for Him, and that He desires our praise?

How do we make praise a priority in our lives?

The answer comes as we grow in prayer. When we pray, we are focusing our attention on the One who is worthy of our praise.

Psalm 95 (verses 1–2, 6–7) invites us to worship the Lord.

Come, let us sing for joy to the LORD;
let us shout aloud to the Rock of our salvation.
Let us come before him with thanksgiving
and extol him with music and song....

Come, let us bow down in worship,
let us kneel before the LORD our Maker;
for he is our God
and we are the people of his pasture.

Psalm 100 is another powerful praise psalm.

Shout for joy to the LORD, all the earth.
Worship the LORD with gladness;
come before him with joyful songs.
Know that the LORD is God.
It is he who made us, and we are his;
we are his people, the sheep of his pasture.

Enter his gates with thanksgiving
and his courts with praise;
give thanks to him and praise his name.
For the LORD is good and his love endures forever;
His faithfulness continues through all generations.

What a precious promise by a faithful Father. He
assures us that His faithfulness will continue through all
generations!

May your heart be blessed and reassured of His promises. May His peace and joy overflow within you as you pray, sing, or shout Psalm 150:

Praise the LORD.

Praise God in his sanctuary;
praise him in his mighty heavens.
Praise him for his acts of power;
praise him for his surpassing greatness.
Praise him with the sounding of the trumpet,
praise him with the harp and lyre,
praise him with timbrel and dancing,
praise him with the strings and pipe,
praise him with the clash of cymbals,
praise him with resounding cymbals.

Let everything that has breath praise the LORD.

Praise the LORD.

In the psalms above, highlight in RED what speaks to your heart. Highlight in YELLOW what God might be inviting you to do. Highlight in BLUE God's promises.

Hymn of Praise

REFLECTION

It didn't take long to choose the hymn for this theme. How many of us have been in gatherings where this timeless song concluded the worship, or have sat around in an intimate gathering of family and friends that broke into song, praising God for His every blessing? Mary and Elizabeth are beautiful examples of how we can encourage and edify one another while praising God and thanking Him for His surpassing greatness and power.

Whether you choose to read and meditate on the words, sing along with a recording, or worshipfully dance to the music, may your heart be stirred, and your soul filled.

PRAISE GOD, FROM WHOM ALL BLESSINGS FLOW
1674, Thomas Ken

Praise God from whom all blessings flow;
Praise Him, all creatures here below;
Praise Him above, ye heav'nly host;
Praise Father, Son, and Holy Ghost.
Amen.

DAY 4

Digging Deeper

STUDY

One of the most beautiful acts of worship is found in Mark 14:3–9. In the New International Version, the title reads, "Jesus Anointed at Bethany."

A Pharisee named Simon invited Jesus to have dinner with him and some other guests. What follows is a summary of that special encounter.

"While he was in Bethany, reclining at the table in the home of Simon the Leper, a woman came with an alabaster jar of very expensive perfume, made of pure nard. She broke the jar and poured the perfume on his head.

Some of those present were saying indignantly to one another, 'Why this waste of perfume? It could have been sold for more than a year's wages and the money given to the poor.' And they rebuked her harshly.

'Leave her alone,' said Jesus. 'Why are you bothering her? She has done a beautiful thing to me. The poor you will always have with you, and you can help them any time you want. But you will not always have me. She did what she could. She poured perfume on my body beforehand to prepare for my burial. Truly

I tell you, wherever the gospel is preached throughout the world, what she has done will also be told, in memory of her" (Mark 14:3–9).

Matthew and Luke also recorded their versions of this story. Luke noted in Luke 7:9 that the Pharisees recognized her as a woman who lived a sinful life and judged Jesus for allowing her to anoint His feet.

"'If this man were a prophet, he would know who is touching him and what kind of woman she is—that she is a sinner.' Jesus responded with a story. 'Two people owed money to a certain moneylender. One owed him five hundred denarii, and the other fifty. Neither of them had the money to pay him back, so he forgave the debts of both. Now which of them will love him more?'

Simon replied, 'I suppose the one who had the bigger debt forgiven.'

'You have judged correctly,' Jesus said.

Then he turned toward the woman and said to Simon, 'Do you see this woman? I came into your house. You did not give me any water for my feet, but she wet my feet with her tears and wiped them with her hair. You did not give me a kiss, but this woman from the time I entered, has not stopped kissing my feet. You did not put oil on my head, but she has poured perfume on my feet. Therefore, I tell you, her many sins have been forgiven—as her great love has shown. But whoever has been forgiven little loves little.'

Then Jesus said to her, 'Yours sins are forgiven'" (Luke 7:39–48).

The Master graciously received this woman's offering of worship and absolved her of all debt, guilt, and shame. What utter inexplicable joy she must have felt.

Do you ever close your eyes and imagine what it would have been like to be in the room with Jesus physically? To worship Him, fellowship with Him, share a meal, or hear His voice audibly?

When Simon sought to belittle this woman's deeds in both passages, one as a waste of money and one as being unworthy to be in the room, Jesus defended and praised her. He went even further, He rebuked Simon for not being a gracious host in following the usual customs of greeting Him with a kiss, washing His feet, and anointing His head with oil.

He applauded the fallen woman, who had probably never received a word of encouragement, affirmation, or praise in her life. Jesus said this nameless woman worshiped and loved much because she had been forgiven much.

We have all been forgiven much. We have all been given the opportunity to worship Jesus and show our love and devotion to Him just as this woman did over two thousand years ago. Are we making time for Jesus? Are we making Him the focus of our lives? Because when we do, abundant blessing will follow.

QUESTIONS

1. How do you think this woman felt when Jesus stood up for her and defended her actions?

....

....

....

....

2. What do you think went through Simon's mind as Jesus rebuked him?

....

....

....

....

3. What were the usual customs for receiving guests in Bible times?

....

....

....

....

....

PRAYER

Dear Heavenly Father, my heart's desire is to love, worship, and adore You. My soul glorifies You, and my spirit rejoices in You, my God and Savior. Thank You for releasing me from my guilt and shame. Thank You for accepting me just as I am. Help me rejoice in You always, in spite of my circumstances. Help me know that You are with me and for me. Help everything that I do, say, think, and feel bring glory to You alone. May my offering of worship be acceptable and pleasing in Your sight. Help me praise You and lead others to praise You, Jesus, because You are good and greatly to be praised.

In Your holy and matchless name, I pray. Amen.

ACTION STEPS

1. What makes worship so appealing to you?

....

....

....

....

....

2. How will you apply this in your daily life?

....

....

....

....

....

3. With whom will you share this truth?

....

....

....

....

....

....

....

CHAPTER 6

COMMITMENT
Mary
Magdalene

MEMORY VERSE

I have been crucified with Christ
and I no longer live, but Christ lives in me.
The life I now live in the body, I live by faith
in the Son of God, who loved me
and gave himself for me.

GALATIANS 2:20

Definition of Commitment

An agreement or pledge to do something in the future

PRAYER

Dear Heavenly Father,
Thank You for loving me and making me Your daughter.
Help me love You with my whole heart.
Help me love others the way You love me.
Thank You for washing away my sins and making me clean.
Help me rejoice in You always, in spite of my circumstances.
I want to follow You as my Lord and Savior.
Fill me with Your Holy Spirit. Make me a woman after
*   Your own heart.*
Make me an instrument of Your grace, truth, and justice.
Use me for Your glory and to be a blessing to others.
Gracious Father, I pray in the name of Jesus Christ our
*   Savior and in the power of the Holy Spirit. Amen.*

STUDY

As you begin the study, carefully read the definition
of *commitment*, pray the daily prayer, and review your
memory verse.

What does it mean to be fully committed to someone
or something? Whether a spouse, a sports activity, or

a cause, commitment is required. All of these require our time, our talents, and our resources. But before we commit, we must engage our hearts. It is a decision of heart and of mind to be an intentional, committed, and sold-out follower of Jesus Christ.

Below is the personal testimony of a dear friend, co-laborer, and passionate follower of Jesus. Her love for Him is contagious, and her story illustrates that often, a relationship with Jesus is not easy or fast. It took ten years of trying to run and hide before Katie let Jesus find her, bring her back home, and take His rightful place as Lord of her life.

KATIE'S STORY

Just how did I find myself sitting alone in a rowboat in the center of a huge storm in Prince William Sound, Alaska? All around me, the wind whipped, and the waves swelled. From that little boat I wept out of sorrow and screamed out of fear into the howling wind. The boat was my life, and the storm was the consequences of my sin and the sins of others harassed me. The waves of guilt and shame were about to crush me when I heard a voice. This voice was kind and assertive, and I had never heard it before. How could twenty-nine years pass without knowing this voice? When it spoke, the storm stopped and I heard the beautiful voice saying, "That's enough, Katie. You are Mine." God the Father was speaking to me by His Holy Spirit. In a vision, I saw a hand grab me out of the boat and set my feet onto high ground. While others saw me as a rebel—wild, flaky, ugly, and worthless—God, my Father, saw me as His precious, rare, vibrant, loyal, and beautiful daughter. The summer of 2009, when I was twenty-nine years old, saw the long-awaited response to prayers from my mother and my great uncle Jerry.

I lived with my great aunt and uncle for a year in 1999 after an episode of abuse led to a failed suicide attempt. My Uncle Jerry tried to show me God the Father's love, but I felt so broken and unable to receive it that I rebelled against this love. One day he sat me down and said, "Honey, I love you and want you to live with us. But if you don't change your behavior, we can't allow you to stay here." The love they were showering me with was so uncomfortable that I chose to leave. I bounced from one broken relationship to the next. For ten years I dodged Uncle Jerry's phone calls.

My uncle was overjoyed when he found out I had an encounter with Jesus. He immediately invited me to enter into a prayer covenant with him: "Would you ask Jesus to be the Lord of your life each day and to change you any way He wants?" The words resonated deep within my soul. I knew that life apart from Jesus was filled with condemnation, emptiness, and futility. "Yes," was my immediate reply. I desperately wanted the presence of Jesus to fill my life with His abundance and beauty. Jerry continued, "When you pray for yourself, Katie, would you be willing to pray for me?" And so began my prayer journey, praying with and for others as we committed to following Jesus together.

The words God spoke to me changed the way I saw myself. I went from worthless in my own eyes to priceless in the eyes of the God of love. Can I just say to those of you who are waiting for those long-awaited prayers to be answered, don't give up! Jesus is with you in the garden of anguish. He hears you and is faithful to respond in His perfect time.

QUESTIONS

1. What did you learn from Katie's story?

....

....

....

....

....

2. Whom in your life do you want to see transformed by the power of God's love?

....

....

....

....

....

3. What does committing every area of your life to Christ mean to you?

....
....
....
....
....

4. What, if anything, is you holding back?

....
....
....
....
....

5. What in you do you want to have Jesus change?

....
....
....
....
....
....
....
....

A Psalm

REFLECTION

Commitment implies an intentional or deliberate action. Commitment is not for the faint of heart, as Katie's story illustrates. You must want it with all your heart and soul. It's a desperate kind of yearning. "Jesus, I want to follow You. Jesus, I'm Yours; do with me as You will—make me more like Yourself, transform me; change me any way You want."

Read Psalm 63. Do you see the desperation in David's prayer? Can you feel his desperate passion to experience God's presence in his life? Do you feel that kind of longing within your heart?

PSALM 63

A psalm of David. When he was in the Desert of Judah.

You, God, are my God,
earnestly I seek you;
I thirst for you,
my whole being longs for you,
In a dry and parched land
where there is no water.

I have seen you in the sanctuary
and beheld your power and your glory.
Because your love is better than life,
my lips will glorify you.
I will praise you as long as I live,
and in your name I will lift up my hands.
I will be fully satisfied as with the richest of foods;
With singing lips my mouth will praise you.

On my bed I remember you;
I think of you through the watches of the night.
Because you are my help,
I sing in the shadow of your wings.
I cling to you;
your right hand upholds me.

In the psalm above, highlight in RED what speaks to your heart.
Highlight in YELLOW what God might be inviting you to do.
Highlight in BLUE God's promises.

Hymn of Praise

REFLECTION

The song "Always Jesus" has spoken poignantly in many of our life stories. "Jesus, the leader of my life, the anchor in the raging seas, the way, the truth, the life." Jesus' kingship demands our commitment to the One who holds us in the palm of His hand and the One who brings us peace.

Whether you choose to read and meditate on the words, sing along with a recording, or worshipfully dance to the music, may your heart be stirred, and your soul filled.

ALWAYS JESUS
2019, by Saddleback Worship

The first name on my lips,
The friend who I can sit with
My daily advocate,
The safety of Your kingship.
You'll always be the reason.
You'll always be enough.
Jesus, always Jesus.
Jesus, always.
Your depth of love for me

Is my anchor in the raging seas.
You speak and You bring peace.
You are always holding me.

You'll always be the reason.
You'll always be enough.
Jesus, always Jesus.
Jesus, always.
Leader of my life,
the door, the way, the vine.
Jesus, always Jesus.
You stand outside of time,
The word, the truth, the life.
Jesus, always Jesus.

Digging Deeper

STUDY

Mary Magdalene understood commitment. She possessed the God-given character attributes that flow from commitment: bravery, faithfulness, strength, and devotion. She was one of the few followers who stood with Mary, Jesus' mother, as He was crucified. She stayed and watched the horror of it. We can only imagine her profound grief in seeing the One who gave her life, the One who mercifully cast out seven demons from her body, the One who found her worthy to serve, and the One who loved her unconditionally, suffering and crying out to His Father.

Commitment requires sacrifice. In Mark 15:40–41, we find Mary Magdalene was one of a group of women who not only followed Jesus, but one who was committed to Him by supporting His work and caring for His needs. So it was not surprising that she would be one of the women who prepared spices for Jesus' body when she visited His tomb (Luke 23:55–56; 24:1).

John's depiction of what happened at the grave is powerful. In John 20:1–18 we get a bird's-eye view of what took place:

"Early on the first day of the week, while it was still dark, Mary Magdalene went to the tomb and saw that the stone had been removed from the entrance. So she came running to Simon Peter and the other disciple, the one Jesus loved, and said, 'They have taken the Lord out of the tomb, and we don't know where they have put him!'

So Peter and the other disciple started for the tomb. Both were running, but the other disciple outran Peter and reached the tomb first. He bent over and looked in at the strips of linen lying there but did not go in. Then Simon Peter came along behind him and went straight into the tomb. He saw the strips of linen lying there, as well as the cloth that had been wrapped around Jesus' head. The cloth was still lying in its place, separate from the linen. Finally the other disciple, who had reached the tomb first, also went inside. He saw and believed. (They still did not understand from Scripture that Jesus had to rise from the dead.) Then the disciples went back to where they were staying" (John 20:1–10).

Mary Magdalene was at the tomb first. She saw the stone rolled away and ran back to tell Peter and John. They accompanied her back to the tomb to find only the strips of cloth that clothed the body of Jesus. Not fully understanding at that moment about the resurrection, they left and went back home. But not Mary.

"Now Mary stood outside the tomb crying. As she wept, she bent over to look into the tomb and saw two angels in white, seated where Jesus' body had been, one at the head and the other at the foot.

They asked her, 'Woman, why are you crying?'

'They have taken my Lord away,' she said, 'and I don't know where they have put him.' At this, she turned around and saw Jesus standing there, but she did not realize that it was Jesus.

He asked her, 'Woman, why are you crying? Who is it you are looking for?'

Thinking he was the gardener, she said, 'Sir, if you have carried him away, tell me where you have put him, and I will get him.'

Jesus said to her, 'Mary.'

She turned toward him and cried out in Aramaic, 'Rabboni!' (which means Teacher).

Jesus said, 'Do not hold on to me, for I have not yet ascended to the Father. Go instead to my brothers and tell them, "I am ascending to my Father and your Father, to my God and your God."'

Mary Magdalene went to the disciples with the news: 'I have seen the Lord!' And she told them that he had said these things to her" (John 20:11–18).

Isn't it amazing that Jesus chose to appear first to a woman? Jesus recognized and rewarded Mary Magdalene's undying love and devotion. He witnessed her gratitude when He healed her of the evil spirits within her—her life dramatically changed because of Jesus' love! Courage and strength replaced fear and torment. And Mary, from that day forward, became a committed follower, in love with her Savior. She followed Him to the cross, then to His tomb, where she was honored by being the first to see her resurrected Lord.

Jesus must have been moved to see her alone, weeping for Him. Jesus, being full of compassion, understood her grief. "Sir, if you have carried him away, tell me where you have put him, and I will get him," she pleaded (verse 15). What utter devotion! And then Jesus' tender response of simply calling her name, "Mary." And at once she recognized the voice of her Healer, her Friend, her Savior, and cried out, "Rabboni!" (verse 16). Could there be any greater reward for what she endured? Her reward was the joy of seeing Jesus face-to-face; of knowing He was indeed alive, and being the very first to hear His tender voice.

Mother Teresa's famous words invite us to experience all that Mary must have felt.

> "'I have called you by your name,' Jesus said. 'You are mine. You are precious in my sight. I love you.' If you love Christ, it will be easy for you to fully belong to Jesus and to give Jesus to everyone you find."

Mary Magdalene was engaged with her Savior's presence; her sin was covered by her life of pure obedience.

The strength of Jesus sustained her in her trials, just as His blessings restored her soul. Mary followed Jesus in life and in death. She understood commitment and obedience. She experienced His comfort in her sorrow—first when He healed her of demon possession and then when He met her at the tomb—her weary soul instantly revived at the sight of Jesus.

You and I can encounter Jesus every day—Jesus, the Healer, the Restorer, the Giver of Life, our Advocate, our Mediator, our Redeemer, our Bread of Life—each time we approach His throne of grace. As you pray, "I want to follow You as my Lord and Savior. Change me any way You want," hear His voice and allow it to minister to the very depths of your soul. Spend time in His presence and allow yourself to sense His nearness. May our faithfulness in prayer be a testimony to Jesus of our love, commitment, and undying devotion.

QUESTIONS

1. What stood out in the story as significant for you?

....

....

2. How is commitment demonstrated in this story?

....

....

3. In what ways are you like Mary Magdalene? In what ways are you different?

....

....

4. Why do you think Jesus chose a woman to be the first to see Him after His resurrection?

....

....

5. Name one thing that is keeping you from being fully committed to Jesus.

....

....

....

....

Prayer

Dear Heavenly Father, the cry of my heart is to please You and bring You joy. Thank You that You call me daughter. Thank You that You draw near when I cry out to You. Have Your perfect way in me. I want to follow You every moment of every day. I surrender myself to You. Be the Lord of my life today and change me any way You want. Fill me with Your Holy Spirit. Glorify Yourself in and through me. Lead me in the way everlasting.

In Jesus' name I pray. Amen.

ACTION STEPS

1. What makes commitment so appealing to you?

....

2. How will you apply this in your daily life?

....

....

3. With whom will you share this truth?

....

....

....

CHAPTER 7

DEPENDENCE

Practicing the Presence of the Holy Spirit

MEMORY VERSE

Do not get drunk on wine, which leads to debauchery.
Instead, be filled with the Spirit, speaking to
one another with psalms, hymns, and songs from
the Spirit. Sing and make music from your heart
to the Lord, always giving thanks to God the Father for
everything, in the name of our Lord Jesus Christ.

EPHESIANS 5:18–20

DAY 1

Definition of Dependence

The quality or state of being influenced
or determined by or subject to another

PRAYER

Dear Heavenly Father,
Thank You for loving me and making me Your daughter.
Help me love You with my whole heart.
Help me love others the way You love me.
Thank You for washing away my sins and making me clean.
Help me rejoice in You always, in spite of my circumstances.
I want to follow You as my Lord and Savior.
Fill me with Your Holy Spirit. Make me a woman after
Your own heart.
Make me an instrument of Your grace, truth, and justice.
Use me for Your glory and to be a blessing to others.
Gracious Father, I pray in the name of Jesus Christ our
Savior and in the power of the Holy Spirit. Amen.

STUDY

As you begin the study, carefully read the definition of
dependence, pray the prayer, and review your memory
verse.

Our society is riddled with all kinds of addictions

like alcohol, drugs, sex, and money. The sad reality is that human society is dependent on these behaviors that seek to fill a void within. Satan's threefold agenda is to seek, to kill, and to destroy. This is not just outside the church, but sadly, inside our churches and homes. What is our defense against the spiritually decaying dependencies that the world offers?

The following testimony is a wonderful example of what it means to be fully dependent upon Christ and submit wholly to His lordship.

A FRIEND'S STORY

Everything looked really good on the outside. We lived in a nice house in a nice neighborhood with our three wonderful kids and a sweet dog. My husband traveled a lot for his work, and I was able to work in the home. All seemed perfect, but was it?

We had some very difficult long-term circumstances in our home. One of our children struggled with mental and emotional issues and learning disabilities that made most days very hard. My husband and I had difficult marital issues. With his frequent travel, I was left to figure out how to get the help our child needed, while caring for our two other children. I began drinking "just to relax" on weekends. Then I decided to drink "to just relax" after a stressful weekday, which turned into many days, until it didn't matter what day it was, and by early evening, almost every evening, I would start drinking "to just relax." It was, in my mind, a reward for a job well-done that day. God, however, did not call this little habit of mine a reward; He called it an addiction and an idol. I was depending on that daily drink or two, instead of Him.

One day, as I was watering the plants on my front porch, I clearly remember God lovingly teaching me of His desire for me to stop drinking. I was mad. Hadn't I given Him everything? Why couldn't He just stay out of this area of my life? I let Him know that I would not comply with His wish in this area of my life. Days went by, and I was miserable. I made an agreement with the Lord. I told myself that I would not drink on weekdays, because certainly He didn't mean to give up drinking on the weekends too! And I tried that plan out for a while.

Then I started redefining the true definition of weekend. Was it Friday through Saturday only, or did it include Sunday? And since Thursday night was so close to Friday, are Thursdays included as part of the weekend? This ridiculous deal-making sadly continued for one year, and I was still miserable. My Bible reading felt dry, and my prayer time was strained. God seemed so distant. I got so sick of myself, I finally turned to God and said He could have it all. I was done bargaining. When I committed to stop drinking for good, He immediately took away any desire I had to drink. I was filled with His peace and felt His Presence. It was glorious!

God knew what lay ahead for me, and in His kindness, He insisted on a clear, sober mind at all times. The darkest days were yet to come, and I would need to rely on His presence, wisdom, and peace, not the numbing escape of alcohol.

QUESTIONS

1. What stood out to you as significant in this story?

....

....

2. In what ways can you relate to her struggle?

....

....

3. Is there something in your life that is keeping you from being fully dependent on Jesus?

....

....

4. What or whom are you dependent upon for happiness?

....

....

....

....

....

....

A Psalm

REFLECTION

As you read through Psalms, one thing that is evident throughout is David's dependence on the presence of God. In fact, he was so sensitive to God's presence in his life that during times when he lost the sense of God's nearness, he pursued it with fury.

Often our reaction to seemingly unanswered prayer, or the feeling that God is distant, is to stop praying. But this is precisely when we must pray on—to keep praying when all is calm and during the storms of life. True dependency is leaning on Jesus not just during the mountaintop experiences but also deep in the valleys. Most often it is in the valleys where we are tested, sharpened, and brought to our knees. We recognize we cannot do it alone. We need the love of our Father, the grace of Jesus, and the fellowship of His Holy Spirit to press on. (See 2 Corinthians 13:14.)

PSALM 13

How long, LORD? Will you forget me forever?
How long will you hide your face from me?
How long must I wrestle with my thoughts
and day after day have sorrow in my heart?
How long will my enemy triumph over me?

Look on me and answer, LORD my God.
Give light to my eyes, or I will sleep in death,
and my enemy will say, "I have overcome him,"
and my foes will rejoice when I fall.

But I trust in your unfailing love;
my heart rejoices in your salvation.
I will sing the LORD's praise,
for he has been good to me.

In the psalm above, highlight in RED what speaks to your heart.
Highlight in YELLOW what God might be inviting you to do.
Highlight in BLUE God's promises.

Hymn of Praise

REFLECTION

The song "Spirit of God" beautifully reminds us to invite the Holy Spirit to take His rightful place in our lives. May our eyes and hearts recognize "his incomparably great power for us who believe" (Ephesians 1:19). As He fills us with His Holy Spirit, may our hearts overflow with gratitude, always giving thanks to God the Father for everything, because in Him, you and I have everything we will ever need.

Whether you choose to read and meditate on the words, sing along with a recording, or worshipfully dance to the music, may your heart be stirred, and your soul filled.

SPIRIT OF GOD
2017, Saddleback Worship

Can you hear it?
A sudden quiet
You cannot deny
When the Spirit rushes in.
The air is changing.

The ground is shaking.
Anticipating His presence here to dwell.

When You fall, when You fall,
All my walls begin to break.

Spirit of God, Spirit of God,
Come and take Your place,
Come and take Your place.
Here in our hearts,
Here in our hearts,
Come and have Your way,
Come and have Your way.

As we're believing, God, You're moving,
The blind are seeing,
Every wound begins to heal.
Would You come in power,
Let Your holy fire awake revival.
Let the place resound with praise.

Digging Deeper

STUDY

> Do not get drunk on wine, which leads to debauchery. Instead, be filled with the Spirit, speaking to one another with psalms, hymns and songs from the Spirit. Sing and make music from your heart to the Lord, always giving thanks to God the Father for everything, in the name of our Lord Jesus Christ. (Ephesians 5:18–20)

Paul instructs that we are to be filled with the Holy Spirit—dependent upon Him each moment of each day. This only comes through prayer. It comes by intentionally asking Him to fill you with His Holy Spirit.

The Holy Spirit is a gift Jesus promised His disciples who would come and minister to them since Jesus would be returning to His Father in heaven. The disciples were dependent upon Jesus. He was their teacher, guide, healer, and best friend. John 14 is a treasure chest of promises Jesus made to them. Imagine the sorrow they were feeling when they found out Jesus would not remain with them! They had yet to encounter and know the power of the Holy Spirit, who would soon come.

As we dig deeper into God's Word, we find many

passages on the Holy Spirit. Below are some passages that will take us on the journey from when Jesus first made the promise to the disciples, to His fulfillment of the promise, and to our invitation to receive His promise.

"And I will ask the Father, and he will give you another advocate to help you and be with you forever—the Spirit of truth. The world cannot accept him, because it neither sees him nor knows him. But you know him, for he lives with you and will be in you. I will not leave you as orphans; I will come to you. Before long, the world will not see me anymore, but you will see me. Because I live, you also will live. On that day you will realize that I am in my Father, and you are in me, and I am in you. Whoever has my commands and keeps them is the one who loves me. The one who loves me will be loved by my Father, and I too will love them and show myself to them" (John 14:16–21).

"All this I have spoken while still with you. But the Advocate, the Holy Spirit, whom the Father will send in my name, will teach you all things and will remind you of everything I have said to you. Peace I leave with you; my peace I give you. I do not give to you as the world gives. Do not let your hearts be troubled and do not be afraid" (John 14:25–27).

"But when he, the Spirit of truth, comes, he will guide you into all the truth" (John 16:13).

Here we see that Jesus promised His disciples a Friend—an Advocate, who would not only be with them, but help them forever! And they knew Jesus always keeps His promises. He always speaks the truth.

Let's review His promises:

- You won't be an orphan.
- I will come to you.
- Because I live, you will live.
- You will be loved.
- I will show Myself to you.
- I will teach you all things.
- I will remind you what you've been taught already.
- I will give you My peace.

After making those promises, He concluded, "Do not let your hearts be troubled and do not be afraid" (John 14:27).

I'm writing this in the midst of the COVID-19 outbreak. The world is in chaos. Many are on lockdown, many have lost jobs, and the stock market dropped significantly. Families have experienced death intimately, and the world is hungry for comfort because the hearts of many are troubled. We know COVID-19 will pass, but we will always be facing different kinds of crises that challenge us to trust the Lord. These turbulent times demand that each of us test ourselves and ask difficult questions.

What am I most dependent upon? My health? My finances? My job or career?

Can I say with confidence, "My God will meet all your needs according to the riches of his glory in Christ Jesus" (Philippians 4:19)?

When you are feeling stressed, discouraged, or frightened, imagine Jesus speaking His promises over you, just like He did to His disciples. Fill in the blanks with your name.

........................., I will not leave you as an orphan.

........................., I will come to you.

........................., because I live, you also will live.

........................., you are loved.

........................., I will show Myself to you.

........................., I will teach you all things.

........................., I will give you My peace.

On Pentecost, not long after Jesus' promise, a strong wind blew, and He filled everyone with His Holy Spirit:

"Suddenly a sound like the blowing of a violent wind came from heaven and filled the whole house where they were sitting. They saw what seemed to be tongues of fire that separated and came to rest on each of them. All of them were filled with the Holy Spirit and began to speak in other tongues as the Spirit enabled them" (Acts 2:2–4).

That same Holy Spirit can dwell inside of each one of us and is ours for the asking. The following verse is my prayer for you.

"May the God of hope fill you with all joy and peace as you trust in him, so that you may overflow with hope by the power of the Holy Spirit" (Romans 15:13).

If we are dependent upon the Holy Spirit, we will be filled with the fruit of His Spirit. How comforting to know that we can be filled with His joy and peace in spite of our circumstances!

We can abound in hope because of the Holy Spirit within us. What an encouragement to know that the Spirit of God is lifting us up to the Father with great passion! He speaks in wordless groans for His children: "In the same way, the Spirit helps us in our weakness. We do not know what we ought to pray for, but the Spirit himself intercedes for us through wordless groans" (Romans 8:26).

And the fruit of the Spirit also live inside each one of us:

> "But the fruit of the Spirit is love, joy, peace, forbearance, kindness, goodness, faithfulness, gentleness and self-control. Against such things there is no law. Those who belong to Christ Jesus have crucified the flesh with its passions and desires. Since we live by the Spirit, let us keep in step with the Spirit. Let us not become conceited, provoking and envying each other" (Galatians 5:22–26).

What a gentle reminder of our need to depend upon Him, each step of the way. The Holy Spirit is our source of power. If you have a lamp that's not plugged in, it is not going to give light. It is the same for you and me. If we are not spending time in prayer, intentionally asking for His Spirit, we run on empty and are unable to bear eternal fruit.

The source of love, joy, peace, patience, kindness, goodness, faithfulness, gentleness, and self-control is found in Jesus and the power of His Holy Spirit. His gift to each one of us is His abiding presence. Prayer is crucial because it is life-giving.

Spending time with Jesus every day must be our number-one priority. Spending time in His Word and spending time in prayer show our dependence upon God the Father, God the Son, and God the Holy Spirit.

QUESTIONS

1. Which of the Bible passages we have read speak to your heart and why?

....

....

2. Write down three of the promises Jesus made to His disciples.

....

....

....

3. What enables us to bear eternal fruit?

....

....

4. When you are filled with the Holy Spirit, how does it make you feel?

....

....

5. What is one thing we can do to be assured we are filled with the Spirit?

....

....

Prayer

Dear Heavenly Father, I thank You and praise You for loving me unconditionally. Thank You for being long-suffering, patient, and kind. Thank You that when I go astray, You are still with me, gently leading me back home. Help me to be utterly dependent upon You through the power of Your Holy Spirit. Come as my Comforter, Teacher, and Guide. Guide me in all areas of my life. Make me a woman after Your own heart who daily seeks after You. Have Your perfect way in me so that You can use me powerfully for Your glory.

In Jesus' name I pray. Amen.

ACTION STEPS

1. What makes dependence on God so appealing to you?

....

2. How will you apply this in your daily life?

....
....

3. With whom will you share this truth?

....
....
....

CHAPTER 8

INFLUENCE
Ministering to the Least of These

MEMORY VERSE

In the same way, let your light shine before others,
that they may see your good deeds
and glorify your Father in heaven.

MATTHEW 5:16

Definition of Influence

The power or capacity of causing an effect
in indirect or intangible ways

PRAYER

Dear Heavenly Father,
Thank You for loving me and making me Your daughter.
Help me love You with my whole heart.
Help me love others the way You love me.
Thank You for washing away my sins and making me clean.
Help me rejoice in You always, in spite of my circumstances.
I want to follow You as my Lord and Savior.
Fill me with Your Holy Spirit. Make me a woman after
  Your own heart.
Make me an instrument of Your grace, truth, and justice.
Use me for Your glory and to be a blessing to others.
Gracious Father, I pray in the name of Jesus Christ our
  Savior and in the power of the Holy Spirit. Amen.

STUDY

As you begin the study, carefully read the definition of
influence, pray the prayer, and review your memory verse.

The following is Anuja's testimony, a dear friend we
met while living in Asia, along with her husband, Deepak.

It's been an incredible blessing to watch their ministry unfold over the decades.

ANUJA'S STORY

As I worked with Campus Crusade for more than fifteen years, I discipled the influencers of society. But after visiting a slum in New Delhi, Jesus was calling me to minister to the least of these.

It began with my visit to the slum where I saw the destitute before my very eyes. Children were playing on the garbage piles with no food, no clothes, and no hope. To them it was simply their unfortunate destiny.

My heart was broken. I began to pray and ask God to show me how I could make a difference in their lives— without resources or expertise. While praying, God gave me the vision to work with the children of the garbage collectors, and I took the idea to church leaders and donors. We rented a small room in that slum and began with fifteen kids. We taught them hygiene, gave them nutritious meals, medical aid, and a basic education for a period of two years.

After that time, we helped them get the proper papers needed to gain admission into the government (public) school. At the same time, we started tutoring centers throughout North India. Today we have one hundred-thirty centers where more than four thousand children come for two hours a day to receive a good education and experience God's love.

You may not have the opportunity to make such a profound impact in our nation, but what might God be calling you to do in your community? Intentionally ask Him and listen for His response.

I love this prayer taken from the ninth edition of the *Book of Common Prayer According to the Use in King's Chapel*, 1986:

"God be in my head and in my understanding;
God be in my eyes and in my looking;
God be in my mouth and in my speaking;
God be in my heart and in my thinking;
God be at my end and at my departing."

QUESTIONS

1. What did you learn from Anuja's story?

....

....

....

....

2. In what parts of your life do you want to see God more?

....

....

....

....

3. What could God be calling you to do in your community?

....

....

....

....

....

....

....

....

God was in Anuja's eyes when she looked upon the slum and saw what Jesus saw. God was in her mouth as she began to share the vision among church leaders and donors. God was in her heart and thinking as she laid plans, hired tutors, and set up the non-formal education centers to minister to the least of these.

We have God's promise that He is with us and for us. And that He will guide our steps if we seek to do His will. "Commit your way to the LORD; trust in him and he will do this: He will make your righteous reward shine like the dawn" (Psalm 37:5–6).

DAY 2

A Psalm

REFLECTION

As you read Psalm 146, ask God to show you ways to minister in your every day. Maybe it's helping in a food pantry, a clothing drive, or a pregnancy care center. Maybe it's serving in the children's ministry at church or tutoring at-risk children. Perhaps it is sharing the Gospel with someone who doesn't know Jesus. Whatever God lays on your heart to do, respond with a "yes"! You may think that you do not have the needed skills or experience—that is often the case for those whom God calls into service. He will guide your steps, one step at a time. He will often take you out of your comfort zone because He wants you to trust Him. He wants your confidence to be in Him alone, and He wants to receive all the glory. Let Him shine in and through you!

PSALM 146:5–10

Blessed are those whose help is the God of Jacob,
whose hope is in the LORD their God.

He is the Maker of heaven and earth,
the sea, and everything in them—

he remains faithful forever.
He upholds the cause of the oppressed
and gives food to the hungry.
The LORD sets prisoners free,
the LORD gives sight to the blind,
the LORD lifts up those who are bowed down,
The LORD loves the righteous.
The LORD watches over the foreigner
and sustains the fatherless and the widow,
but he frustrates the ways of the wicked.

The LORD reigns forever,
your God, O Zion, for all generations.

Praise the LORD.

In the psalm above, highlight in RED what speaks to your heart.
Highlight in YELLOW what God might be inviting you to do.
Highlight in BLUE God's promises.

DAY 3

Hymn of Praise

REFLECTION

This hymn is a prayer inviting Jesus to take every part of us—our whole being—for His eternal purposes. Whether it be our hands, our feet, our voice, or our earthly possessions, when surrendered fully to Jesus, His love will compel us to serve those in our midst and to do so in His strength and for His glory.

Whether you choose to read and meditate on the words, sing along with a recording, or worshipfully dance to the music, may your heart be stirred, and your soul filled.

TAKE MY LIFE AND LET IT BE
1874, Frances R. Havergal

Take my life and let it be
Consecrated, Lord to Thee.
Take my hands and let them move,
at the impulse of Thy love.

Take my feet and let them be
Swift and beautiful for Thee.

Take my voice and let me sing
Always, only, for my King.

Take my lips and let them be
Filled with messages for Thee.
Take my silver and my gold;
Not a mite would I withhold.

Take my love, my God, I pour
At Thy feet its treasure store.
Take myself and I will be
Ever, only, all for Thee.

Digging Deeper

STUDY

As Anuja's story beautifully illustrates, we have tremendous opportunities in our daily life to be instruments of God's grace, truth, and justice. We as Christ's disciples have a profound responsibility in this world. Even within the church there is widespread sexual abuse and use of pornography. All around the world social injustices due to race, gender, religion, or socioeconomic status still exist. Approximately half the children in the world live in poverty. These are all vices and tragedies that darken our world. We are compelled and called, by His matchless example, to be a voice for those who have no voice. "Speak up for those who cannot speak for themselves, for the rights of all who are destitute. Speak up and judge fairly; defend the rights of the poor and needy" (Proverbs 31:8–9).

Jesus' ministry was focused on the oppressed, despised, and rejected of society. He ministered to the impoverished, the sick, the orphan, the unclean—the castoffs. He held women and children in high esteem, even though both groups were often looked down upon and disregarded. Jesus' heart for justice was modeled daily in His ministry and should inspire us to commit to help those who are suffering, the unborn children, the abused, and those who do not know Jesus.

You may ask, "How can I help?" Pray. Show compassion. Share the Gospel. Even if you have the opportunity to influence one person with the love of Christ, it will have an impact.

When you intentionally ask God for opportunities to be His messenger of grace, truth, and justice, trust Him to open unexpected doors and equip you to walk through them. Be bold! Be courageous!

You may not have any idea at this moment how God can and will use you in any given circumstance. Your career may have nothing to do with issues of justice. You may not be serving in ministry or doing nonprofit work. Justice is much bigger than a nonprofit job. Justice is showing that you care for someone who is headed to a godless eternity by sharing the Gospel with them. Justice is intentionally praying by name for people in your life who do not know Jesus, pleading with Him on their behalf. Justice is equipping the next generation to care for the lost like Jesus did.

In Luke 4, you find Jesus reading a passage from Isaiah 61 to the leaders in the synagogue:

> "The Spirit of the Lord is on me,
> because he has anointed me
> to proclaim good news to the poor.
> He has sent me to proclaim freedom for the prisoners

and recovery of sight for the blind,
to set the oppressed free,
to proclaim the year of the Lord's favor" (verses
18–19).

After reading this, He rolled up the scroll, sat down, and declared, "Today this scripture is fulfilled in your hearing" (verse 21).

Jesus was the fulfillment of Isaiah 61. Throughout His ministry on earth, Jesus was healing the sick and the blind, bringing freedom to the oppressed, ministering to the unwanted and accused, and offering hope to the hopeless. He brought His message of life and light to all those He met.

QUESTIONS

1. When in your life have you been on the receiving end of justice or grace that was unexpected? How did it make you feel?

....

....

2. When have you shown grace or justice to someone else that was unexpected, and how did it make you feel?

....

....

3. Share a recent experience of when you shared Christ's message of hope with someone.

....

....

4. How did he/she respond?

....

....

5. What made the interaction effective or not, and what did you learn from it?

....

....

....

DAY 5

Prayer

Dear Heavenly Father, my heart's desire and prayer is that I be an instrument of Your grace, truth, and justice. Give me Your eyes to see the world as You see it. Give me Your heart for those around me. Give me boldness to be a voice for those who have no voice, for those suffering injustices in our world today. Open doors of opportunity to use me as a messenger of Your Gospel of grace. Love through me. Forgive through me. Serve through me. Be my hands and feet. Let Your light shine in and through me so You will be glorified in all I do and say.

In Your precious name I pray. Amen.

ACTION STEPS

1. What makes influence so appealing to you?

....

....

....

....

2. How will you apply this in your daily life?

....

....

....

....

3. With whom will you share this truth?

....

....

....

....

....

....

....

....

....

....

CHAPTER 9

DISCIPLESHIP
The Woman at the Well

MEMORY VERSE

Therefore, go and make disciples of all nations,
baptizing them in the name of the Father and of
the Son and of the Holy Spirit, teaching them to obey
everything I have commanded you. And surely I am
with you always, to the very end of the age.

MATTHEW 28:19–20

Definition of Discipleship

the condition or situation of being a disciple,
a follower, or a student of some philosophy,
especially a follower of Christ

PRAYER

Dear Heavenly Father,
Thank You for loving me and making me Your daughter.
Help me love You with my whole heart.
Help me love others the way You love me.
Thank You for washing away my sins and making me clean.
Help me rejoice in You always, in spite of my circumstances.
I want to follow You as my Lord and Savior.
Fill me with Your Holy Spirit. Make me a woman after
*   Your own heart.*
Make me an instrument of Your grace, truth, and justice.
Use me for Your glory and to be a blessing to others.
Gracious Father, I pray in the name of Jesus Christ our
*   Savior and in the power of the Holy Spirit. Amen.*

STUDY

As you begin the study, carefully read the definition of
discipleship, pray the prayer, and review your memory
verse.

The Great Commission was Jesus' last command. In Matthew 28:18–20, He declared:

"All authority in heaven and on earth has been given to me. Therefore go and make disciples of all nations, baptizing them in the name of the Father and of the Son and of the Holy Spirit, and teaching them to obey everything I have commanded you. And surely I am with you always, to the very end of the age."

So how do we make Jesus' last command a priority in our own lives? Paul offers guidance in Ephesians 6.

"And pray in the Spirit on all occasions with all kinds of prayers and requests. With this in mind, be alert and always keep on praying for all the Lord's people. Pray also for me, that whenever I speak, words may be given me so that I will fearlessly make known the mystery of the gospel" (Ephesians 6:18–19).

If there was ever a time for the Church to rise up and share the hope of the Gospel, it is now. We can do that by the power of the Holy Spirit living inside of us. Intentionally pray and ask God to open doors of opportunity to share with others. Pray, as Paul instructs, that His Holy Spirit will give you the right words as you share, and then pray for that person specifically by name. You will be amazed how God shows up and answers your request. His Holy Spirit will empower you. He will give you the right words. He will speak through you and pray through you.

Remind yourself of God's heart for the world, the world He so loved that He willingly gave His life.

"Greater love has no one than this: to lay down one's life for one's friends" (John 15:13).

"The Lord is not…wanting anyone to perish, but everyone to come to repentance" (2 Peter 3:9).

"He who did not spare his own Son, but gave him up for us all—how will he not also, along with him, graciously give us all things?" (Romans 8:32).

"'Everyone who calls on the name of the Lord will be saved.' How, then, can they call on the one they have not believed in? And how can they believe in the one of whom they have not heard? And how can they hear without someone preaching to them?" (Romans 10:13–14).

Even though many of us live in free countries, we often are afraid to share our faith. Our stomach gets tied up in knots. We think of multiple excuses why we are unable: I have never been to seminary… Evangelism isn't my gifting… I don't know what to say…

Simply pray. "Lord Jesus, please give me the opportunity to share Your message of love with .... Give me the right words so that I will clearly share the Gospel message without fear."

Do you think Jesus will answer your prayer? Absolutely! Ask yourself these questions:

Is it His will that you share the Gospel with others?

Do you trust Him to open doors of opportunity?

Are you willing to step out in faith and trust His leading?

Imagine you have been sentenced to death with no hope of being set free, pardoned, or rescued. You are locked in a cell, far from home. You are alone, terrified, exhausted, and weeping. But then a total stranger enters your life. "Don't be afraid. I came just for you. I am here to set you free. I am here to take your penalty. I am willing to die for you, to give my life so you can live, and not just live but experience abundant life. Because I love you, I will take your penalty and die for you." Would this sacrificial gift compel you to share it with anyone and everyone you met?

QUESTIONS

1. What, if anything, holds you back from sharing your faith?

....

....

....

....

2. How might you initiate a conversation that could lead to sharing your faith?

....

....

....

....

3. Can you write down two to three names of individuals you have felt compelled to share your faith with and commit to doing so in the near future?

....

....

....

....

....

....

....

DAY 2

A Psalm

REFLECTION

Prayer and evangelism are integrally linked together. We cannot accomplish one without the other. Often, I have found myself frightened to speak up and begin a Gospel-centered conversation with someone at the salon, at the grocery store, or with a workman helping at our home. I stop and immediately ask for Jesus to give me the boldness and the words to share. Most times it has resulted in my praying with and for them for a pressing need or concern. God has given us a message of hope, and we must ask Him for a burning desire to share that hope with all we meet.

Psalm 96 is a powerful psalm. More than ever, in this age of technology, God is being exalted as His salvation is being proclaimed every day throughout the world, to almost every tribe, tongue, nation, and people. What unspeakable joy is ours when we take the time to share the Gospel message with even one person! It is both a privilege and a responsibility as followers of Christ to lead others to follow Him too.

PSALM 96

Sing to the LORD a new song;
sing to the LORD, all the earth.

Sing to the LORD, praise his name;
proclaim his salvation day after day.
Declare his glory among the nations,
his marvelous deeds among all peoples.

For great is the LORD and most worthy of praise;
he is to be feared above all gods.
For all the gods of the nations are idols,
but the LORD made the heavens.
Splendor and majesty are before him;
strength and glory are in his sanctuary.

Ascribe to the LORD, all you families of nations,
ascribe to the LORD glory and strength.
Ascribe to the LORD the glory due his name;
bring an offering and come into his courts.
Worship the LORD in the splendor of his holiness;
tremble before him, all the earth.
Say among the nations, "The LORD reigns."
The world is firmly established, it cannot be moved;
he will judge the peoples with equity.

Let the heavens rejoice, let the earth be glad;
let the sea resound, and all that is in it.
Let the fields be jubilant, and everything in them;
let all the trees of the forest sing for joy.
Let all creation rejoice before the LORD, for he comes,
he comes to judge the earth.

He will judge the world in righteousness
and the peoples in his faithfulness.

In the psalm above, highlight in RED what speaks to your heart.
Highlight in YELLOW what God might be inviting you to do.
Highlight in BLUE God's promises.

DAY 3

Hymn of Praise

REFLECTION

Saddleback Worship knocked it out of the ballpark with this courageous call to go. May God give each one of us His passion for reaching the lost.

Jesus said in Matthew 24:14, "And this gospel of the kingdom will be preached in the whole world as a testimony to all nations, and then the end will come."

Whether you choose to read and meditate on the words, sing along with a recording, or worshipfully dance to the music, may your heart be stirred, and your soul filled.

WE MUST GO
2019, by Saddleback Worship

We must go
To stand in for the shamed
For the cause of His great name
We must go

We must go
To go befriend the lost

Carriers of peace at all cost
We must go

To every corner of the earth
Until the day we're called home

Be the hope
Be the light
To the ends of the earth
To the ends of the earth

Be the voice
Be the love
To the ends of the earth
To the ends of the earth

We must go
To souls both far and close
For the ones He died and rose
We must go

To every corner of the earth
Until the day we're called home

Be the hope
Be the light
To the ends of the earth
To the ends of the earth

Be the voice
Be the love
To the ends of the earth
To the ends of the earth

Greater things
Are still to come
In Jesus' name
In Jesus' name

Heaven come,
Your will be done
In Jesus' name
In Jesus' name

Digging Deeper

STUDY

I love the way Jesus ministered to men, women, and children throughout His ministry. He didn't begin by saying, "You're a sinner. Repent. Pray this prayer and you'll be saved." Quite the opposite. He engaged by asking meaningful questions. He listened. He showed compassion. He offered forgiveness, and then He challenged them to follow Him. It's a beautiful model for us to follow.

In John 4, we find the story of Jesus and the Samaritan woman. Jesus was traveling from Judea to Galilee but had to go through Samaria. He was tired and took a rest by Jacob's well. Jesus asked a Samaritan woman for some water.

She was stunned. "You are a Jew and I am a Samaritan woman. How can you ask me for a drink?" (John 4:9) Samaritans were looked down upon by the Jews—and she was also a woman—and women were not valued.

In verse 10, Jesus begins to answer her: "If you knew the gift of God and who it is that asks you for a drink, you would have asked him and he would have given you living water." At first, she did not understand. Jesus went on, "Everyone who drinks this water will be thirsty again, but whoever drinks the water I give them will never thirst. Indeed, the water I give them will become in them a spring of water welling up to eternal life" (verse 13–14).

The woman replied, "Sir, give me this water so that I won't get thirsty and have to keep coming here to draw water" (John 4:15).

Jesus asked her to go and bring her husband. She honestly replied that she did not have one. Jesus said to her in verse 17, "You are right when you say you have no husband. The fact is, you have had five husbands, and the man you now have is not your husband. What you have just said is quite true."

How would this man know this about me? she must have thought. She recognized He was a prophet.

Jesus went on, "You Samaritans worship what you do not know; we worship what we do know, for salvation is from the Jews. Yet a time is coming and has now come when the true worshipers will worship the Father in the Spirit and in truth, for they are the kind of worshipers the Father seeks. God is spirit and his worshipers must worship in the Spirit and in truth" (verses 22–24).

The woman affirmed, "I know that Messiah [called Christ] is coming. When he comes, he will explain everything to us" (verse 25).

Jesus responded, "I, the one speaking to you—I am he" (verse 26).

Imagine her astonishment! This was no ordinary Jewish man; this was the Messiah Himself!

Jesus ministered to women with understanding, compassion, and tenderness. The Church has at times, both past and present, treated those who need a physician, those for whom Jesus died, with judgment and reproach. When she answered honestly that she had five husbands, Jesus did not condemn or belittle her; He did not cast her aside and say, "You're a sinner, I can't associate with you." He met her where she was. He treated her with dignity. When she responded honestly, He commended her for speaking the truth.

Although she was an outcast, simply fetching her daily water when others were not around, Jesus didn't look down on her. He looked into her heart and into her very soul. He knew she craved more than physical water. She craved hope. She craved love. She craved acceptance. She craved peace and the spiritual life-giving water that only the Messiah could give. Those few minutes at the well filled her soul with inexplicable joy and caused her to immediately tell others what she experienced.

QUESTIONS

1. What stood out as significant to you in this story?

....

....

....

....

2. What makes Jesus' approach as He ministered to the Samaritan woman so effective?

....

....

....

....

3. How can we be more like Jesus as we approach those who might not know Him?

....

....

....

....

....

....

....

....

Prayer

Dear Heavenly Father, I come before You with a heart full of praise and thanksgiving for Your grace and goodness in my life. Thank You for Your eternal promises to those who believe. Thank You for being my refuge, my fortress, and my God in whom I trust. Thank You for Your great and overwhelming love for me. I ask that You allow Your love to pour through me. Use me for Your glory to boldly share Your message of love with all I meet. Guard my heart from distractions and anything that keeps me from loving You with my whole heart. Guide my steps to walk in Your perfect will. Give me words to speak of Your unfailing kindness and gift of hope. I lift up the nations to You and ask that You will raise up messengers to proclaim Your good news. I ask that Your glory will be seen throughout the nations. That every boy, girl, man, and woman will have an opportunity to hear the story of Jesus, and to receive Your gift to be forever changed.

In the name of Jesus, I pray. Amen.

ACTION STEPS

1. What makes discipleship so appealing to you?

....

....

....

....

2. How will you apply this in your daily life?

....

....

....

....

3. With whom will you share this truth?

....

....

....

....

....

....

....

....

....

....

CHAPTER 10

AUTHORITY
The Woman with the Issue of Blood

MEMORY VERSE

Therefore God exalted him to the highest place
and gave him the name that is above every name,
that at the name of Jesus every knee should bow,
in heaven and on earth and under the earth,
and every tongue acknowledge that
Jesus Christ is Lord, to the glory of God the Father.

PHILIPPIANS 2:9–11

Definition of Authority

Power to influence or command thought,
opinion, or behavior

PRAYER

Dear Heavenly Father,
Thank You for loving me and making me Your daughter.
Help me love You with my whole heart.
Help me love others the way You love me.
Thank You for washing away my sins and making me clean.
Help me rejoice in You always, in spite of my circumstances.
I want to follow You as my Lord and Savior.
Fill me with Your Holy Spirit. Make me a woman after
    Your own heart.
Make me an instrument of Your grace, truth, and justice.
Use me for Your glory and to be a blessing to others.
Gracious Father, I pray in the name of Jesus Christ our
    Savior and in the power of the Holy Spirit. Amen.

STUDY

As you begin the study, carefully read the definition of
authority, pray the prayer, and review your memory verse.

What does the word *authority* conjure up in your
mind when you think of God? Think about these traits
of God:

How He spoke the world into existence (Genesis 1; Isaiah 40:28)

His omniscience (Psalm 139:1–4; Isaiah 46:9–10; Matthew 10:30)

His omnipresence (Psalm 114:7; Matthew 18:20; Colossians 1:17)

His omnipotence (Luke 1:37; Matthew 19:26)

Think about His authority over:

Death (John 11:24–25; 38–44; Acts 26:8; Revelation 1:18)

Disease (Matthew 4:23; Luke 8:43–48; Luke 17:11–19)

Satan (Matthew 4:1–11; Luke 10:19)

This dear sister's story is a magnificent declaration and summation of who God is—His authority, His power, and His majesty.

A FRIEND'S STORY

Whenever I hear the word *authority*, I bristle. In full disclosure, I have struggled with the notion of authority to some degree in every single season of my walk with God. I have always been headstrong, opinionated, passionate, bold, fond of adventure, excited to meet new people and learn absolutely everything I can. I like to be in control of myself—and sometimes others—if I am not mindful.

Growing up, I knew Jesus and was blessed to attend a church where reading, studying, and meditating on the Word was encouraged, even for children. I had a Ryrie Study Bible by the time I was ten years old. I read all about the God who came down on a mountain covered in fire to meet with Moses and to make a forever covenant with His chosen people. I read of prophets whose lives truly were not their own as they were called to be living testimonies and signposts of the Holy God they served. Their lives were uprooted as they found themselves naked, hated, imprisoned, married to adulterers, and living in deserts, caves, and the houses of widows. I saw how Jesus fulfilled everything in the Old Testament and literally carried it into the New Testament by the very words of His mouth. Jesus truly is the radiance of His glory and the exact representation of His nature, upholding all things by the word of His power (Hebrews 1:3).

I fell in love with this God, and at a very deep level knew that to follow Him truly, completely, and absolutely meant absolute abandonment to Him. He is terrifying in His holiness, beautiful in His splendor, and awesome in His power. His authority is absolute, paramount, and unrivaled. Yet when He called me in His authority, I bristled. Not in the normal, eye-rolling way, but in the sheer terror of the majesty and the absolute power of the One who called me. Did I truly believe that He is who He says He is? Do I really believe I am who He says I am?

When I behold the glorious, sovereign God of the Universe who had me in mind before the creation of the world—the God who knitted me together in my mother's womb, who spoke the very world into being, who always was, is, and forever will be, who created every single star in the heavens and has named every one of them, who thunders when He speaks and rides the clouds as chariots, who came to the earth, taking on the form of a man for all of eternity in order to rescue me from every single sin I would ever commit centuries before I was even born—my mind reels with His magnitude. This God who walked as a man on the very earth I live on, who ate food, slept, and came as an infant, weak and vulnerable, was the very picture of profound humility. This God, this man, died a brutal death at the hands of those He came to save! He was sinless, abandoned, beaten, naked, and nailed to a cross of splintery wood. This Son of Man, whose last breath caused the veil between me and my Father God to be torn forever, allowed me a full and direct access to Him. When I behold this Man, I tremble. I weep in gratitude. And I recognize that by His authority I will say "yes" every time. And in His authority, I will cast out demons, heal the sick, and feed the poor. I will go. I will leave my home. I will leave my family. I will go to the ends of the earth declaring His goodness, His staggering kindness, and the audacity of a God who left heaven—heaven!—to come to our rescue. I will go until everyone, everywhere, hears this marvelous and glorious news!

When He called me, He asked that I give Him everything. His authority begs a response of total, absolute abandonment and surrender. And His loving-kindness, His sacrifice, His beauty, and His mercy ensure that He is worth it, and that when I lose my life to Him—in Him—I will actually find it (Matthew 10:39). He imparts His goodness to me. He gives me His authority. When I move in Him, by Him, through Him, and for Him, He moves mountains and raises the dead. He fulfills every single promise and every desire of my heart—even those desires I never even knew I had. His authority actually changes my heart.

When this Man calls, what answer could there possibly be than "YES! YES! YES! Oh, YES, my JESUS, YES!" And so the adventure begins.

QUESTIONS

1. What emotions stir up inside of you when you think of authority?

2. What does God's authority mean to you?

....

....

3. What does authority look like in your life?

....

....

4. Where do you find it challenging to submit to God's authority in your life?

....

....

....

5. How have you submitted to God's authority when it's been against your own desire or will?

....

....

....

6. Write an example of how you felt when your authority was questioned or not followed.

....

....

....

DAY 2

A Psalm

REFLECTION

As the previous testimony so eloquently shared, Psalm 139 speaks of God's authority—His omniscience and omnipresence—in a very personal way to its readers. Our Creator, the all-powerful, all-knowing God of the universe, knows us intimately, better than we know ourselves because He created our inmost being, He knit us together in our mother's womb.

In this psalm, David had a revelation of the joy God had in His heart for him. Be encouraged! God's heart for each one of us is full of joy when He thinks about us and the plan He has for us. Our purpose should be to bring our Father joy; and as we live, move, and have our being in His authority, He fills us with His joy.

As you read through this psalm may you be assured of His presence, power, and authority in your life. Share it with others. Read it to your children. It will reassure them and bring great comfort in the knowledge that God is always with them. How soothing are the words, "If I go up to the heavens, you are there; if I make my bed in the depths, you are there… If I say, 'Surely the darkness will hide me and the light become night around me,' even the darkness will not be dark to you; the night will

177

shine like the day, for darkness is as light to you" (verses 8–12).

May His light purify you and lead you in the way everlasting.

PSALM 139
For the director of music. Of David. A psalm.

You have searched me, LORD,
and you know me.
You know when I sit and when I rise;
you perceive my thoughts from afar.
You discern my going out and my lying down;
you are familiar with all my ways.
Before a word is on my tongue
you, LORD, know it completely.
You hem me in behind and before,
and you lay your hand upon me.
Such knowledge is too wonderful for me,
too lofty for me to attain.

Where can I go from your Spirit?
Where can I flee from your presence?
If I go up to the heavens, you are there;
if I make my bed in the depths, you are there.
If I rise on the wings of the dawn,
if I settle on the far side of the sea,
even there your hand will guide me,

your right hand will hold me fast.
If I say, "Surely the darkness will hide me
and the light become night around me,"
even the darkness will not be dark to you;
the night will shine like the day,
for darkness is as light to you.

For you created my inmost being;
you knit me together in my mother's womb.
I praise you because I am fearfully and wonderfully
made;
your works are wonderful,
I know that full well.
My frame was not hidden from you
when I was made in the secret place,
when I was woven together in the depths of the earth.
Your eyes saw my unformed body;
all the days ordained for me were written in your book
before one of them came to be.
How precious to me are your thoughts, God!
How vast is the sum of them!
Were I to count them,
they would outnumber the grains of sand—
when I awake, I am still with you.

If only you, God, would slay the wicked!
Away from me, you who are bloodthirsty!
They speak of you with evil intent;

your adversaries misuse your name.
Do I not hate those who hate you, LORD,
and abhor those who are in rebellion against you?
I have nothing but hatred for them;
I count them my enemies.
Search me, God, and know my heart;
test me and know my anxious thoughts.
See if there is any offensive way in me,
and lead me in the way everlasting.

In the psalm above, highlight in RED what speaks to your heart.
Highlight in YELLOW what God might be inviting you to do.
Highlight in BLUE God's promises.

Hymn of Praise

REFLECTION

"All Hail the Power of Jesus' Name" beautifully illustrates our heart posture toward Jesus in this hymn. "The name that is above every name" (Philippians 2:9).

Faithful. True. "He is far above all rule and authority, power and dominion, and every name that is invoked, not only in the present age but also in the one to come" (Ephesians 1:21).

As the angels in heaven bow before King Jesus, you and I can join the everlasting song and crown Him Lord of all!

Can there be any more beautiful name deserving of our love? Our praise? Our adoration?

Whether you choose to read and meditate on the words, sing along with a recording, or worshipfully dance to the music, may your heart be stirred, and your soul filled.

Written in 1779 by Edward Perronet, this great hymn of the faith praises the One worthy of all our praise.

ALL HAIL THE POWER OF JESUS' NAME
1779, Edward Perronet

All hail the power of Jesus' name!
Let angels prostrate fall;
Bring forth the royal diadem,
And crown Him Lord of all;
Bring for the royal diadem and crown Him Lord of all.

Let every kindred, every tribe, On this terrestrial ball,
To Him all majesty ascribe,
And crown Him Lord of all;
To Him all majesty ascribe,
And crown Him Lord of all.

O that with yonder sacred throng,
We at His feet may fall!
We'll join the everlasting song,
And crown Him Lord of all;
We'll join the everlasting song,
And crown Him Lord of all.

Digging Deeper

STUDY

Jesus often demonstrated His authority over sickness and disease when He healed the afflicted. The book of Mark records the moving story of the woman with an issue of blood. She had suffered with this condition for twelve years. There seemed to be no cure. She had spent all her money on doctors in the hope she would be cured, but instead of being healed, her condition continued to get worse.

> "A woman was there who had been subject to bleeding for twelve years. She had suffered a great deal under the care of many doctors and had spent all she had, yet instead of getting better she grew worse. When she heard about Jesus, she came up behind him in the crowd and touched his cloak, because she thought, 'If I just touch his clothes, I will be healed.' Immediately her bleeding stopped and she felt in her body that she was freed from her suffering.
>
> At once Jesus realized that power had gone out from him. He turned around in the crowd and asked, 'Who touched my clothes?'
>
> 'You see the people crowding against you,' his

disciples answered, 'and yet you can ask, "Who touched me?"' But Jesus kept looking around to see who had done it. Then the woman, knowing what had happened to her, came and fell at his feet and, trembling with fear, told him the whole truth. He said to her, 'Daughter, your faith has healed you. Go in peace and be freed from your suffering'" (Mark 5:25–34).

This nameless woman understood Jesus' authority. Mark tells us that when she heard about Jesus, and His power to heal, "she came up behind him in the crowd and touched his cloak, because she thought, 'If I just touch his clothes, I will be healed'" (verses 27–28). This woman possessed great faith. She extended her hand to simply touch Jesus' garment and she was immediately healed. Mark writes, "Immediately her bleeding stopped and she felt in her body that she was freed from her suffering" (verse 29).

Jesus knew someone had touched Him because the passage reads, "At once Jesus realized that power had gone out from him. He turned around in the crowd and asked, 'Who touched my clothes?'" (verse 30). I have to laugh reading the disciples' response to Jesus' question. "Jesus, you're standing in the middle of a huge crowd! How can You ask, 'Who touched My clothes?'" (paraphrase).

The woman immediately fell at Jesus' feet. She was frightened and trembling with fear, and told Him what happened. I love Jesus' compassionate response, "Daughter, your faith has healed you. Go in peace and be freed from your suffering" (verse 34).

Jesus, the name above all names, the One to whom all authority has been given, our Healer, our Redeemer, our Advocate, our Friend. Jesus filled this woman with His power when He healed her. He filled her with His love when He acknowledged her presence and her need. "The LORD is near to all who call on him, to all who call on him in truth. He fulfills the desires of those who fear him; he hears their cry and saves them" (Psalm 145:18–19).

When we come to Jesus, when we surrender ourselves to His authority, He graciously extends His hand, He calls us daughter, and He fills us to overflowing with His love and power.

QUESTIONS

1. What significance does the woman's story in Mark 5 have for you?

....

....

....

2. How does Jesus' response reflect His character?

....

....

....

3. How might this story relate to your life or the life of someone you know?

....
....
....

4. If you could meet Jesus face-to-face, what would you ask of Him?

....
....
....

5. What are you trusting Him for right now?

....
....
....

We have read two powerful testimonies from two extraordinary women of God. One present day, and one from two millennia ago. Two women in love with Jesus. Two women who embraced His authority. Two women fully committed to the One who called them by name knowing that salvation is found in no one else, because there is no other name under heaven given to mankind by which we could be saved. Each one of us has access to His authority. Each one of us has a story to tell.

DAY 5

Prayer

Dear Heavenly Father, I thank You and praise You that there is no other name under heaven that we can call on to be saved. Thank You that Your authority over death has brought me life. Thank You that Your authority has made me Your dearly loved daughter, empowered me to walk in Christlikeness, filled me with the fruit of Your Spirit, and invited me to rule and reign with You throughout eternity! Almighty God, Your Word declares that You have given us authority to overcome all the power of the enemy. Help me to grasp the breadth of Your power and recognize Your authority both in and through me.

In Jesus' name I pray. Amen.

ACTION STEPS

1. What makes authority so appealing to you?

....

....

....

....

....

2. How will you apply this in your daily life?

....

....

....

....

....

3. With whom will you share this truth?

....

....

....

....

....

....

....

....

Conclusion

My prayer is that as you have worked through this study, your heart has been encouraged to approach God's throne of grace with boldness and confidence. "I will never leave you or forsake you" is a promise we have from a faithful Father who keeps His promises. Amidst the trials and hurdles in life, we must cling to the One who "took up our pain and bore our suffering" (Isaiah 53:4).

Prayer covenants are a beautiful way to commit to pray for others. Whether praying for your spouse, children, friends, or even a new acquaintance, what better way to strengthen and edify one another than praying the will of God for that person every day for an agreed period of time? It invites the presence and power of the Holy Spirit in ways you never expected and enriches your relationship with whomever you choose to pray. How is God changing me? How is He changing you? These are simple questions that allow you to celebrate and experience God's delight in and through you. "Taste and see that the LORD is good" (Psalm 34:8)!

This last story is written by my daughter, Maria Marballi. My heart carried untold grief when I found out what my father had been doing and how Maria tried to protect the family by hiding it for so many years. What Satan meant for evil, God used for good. Watching how God healed her, trading beauty for ashes, and anointing her to minister to so many, is a testimony of His grace, love and compassion.

MARIA'S STORY

Growing up, I had faith like a child. Before I fell asleep, I brought God every concern, every hope, every request. I knew nothing but the attentiveness of a caring and kind heavenly Father. I knew answered prayers, peaceful nights, and joyful mornings. My parents taught me about a Father who always listened, who always forgave, and who had adopted me as His own. Thanks to them, I knew the source of my provision and peace. This truth prepared me for the trials ahead.

From ages nine to twelve, I was sexually abused by my grandfather when I stayed with him and my grandmother during the summers. Even the most loving parents cannot protect a child from the inevitable suffering that results from a fallen world. But because they taught me that He cared, I brought Him my pain, expectantly awaiting His comfort. And God, rich in mercy, provided peace that the world could not provide.

While my brain coped with the abuse through disassociation and attempts at forgetting about the encounters, one day in particular was different. After an abusive encounter, I was filled with emotions that I could not ignore nor suppress. I went outside for fresh air, and I did what I had forgotten I could do. I brought Jesus my suffering. I asked Him to take away the pain and the emotions. I asked for Him to heal whatever was wrong in my heart. Within moments, He removed it all. As soon as I made my request known, He graciously answered, and the present pain was gone. In the midst of my abuse, God performed a miracle.

I remember that day as a marker of His faithfulness in my life. It reminds me of His goodness and love, that He would come to heal His daughter with immediacy and power. This does not mean that the suffering was altogether resolved in one moment. I have pursued counseling, and still see the impacts of abuse in my life today. God did not remove the trial; but rather He provides daily peace and deliverance from the emotional consequences of evil. He provides comfort and joy along the difficult and long road of recovery.

Years later, I asked Him to use my life for good, that I might share in the suffering of others and bring the light and life of Jesus into the broken parts of others' lives. I asked Him for opportunities, and He continued to answer prayers.

As a college student, God filled my life with freshmen women who knew childhoods of abuse, and allowed me to journey through healing with them, offering the joy and peace from knowing Jesus and walking closely with Him. Today, these women have shepherded many more survivors of abuse, and have brought love and laughter to suffering, and we have all stood and watched as the darkness passed away.

I then asked the Lord for an opportunity to spend my working hours contributing to the work of justice for abused men, women, and children. He answered again, and faithfully provided me with a job in which I can use my gifts to help bring healing, justice, and hope to survivors of human trafficking in Ohio.

This is the power of prayer in my life. He has met my pain with comfort, my sadness with joy, and my questions with guidance. When I called out to Him, He answered. He redeemed the ugliness of abuse and has allowed me to tell of His faithfulness and provision so that He might be glorified, even in the darkness.

What an encouragement to know God redeems our lives from the pit, He crowns us with His loving-kindness and compassion, and He walks with us through mountaintops and valleys. He restores what has been broken.

REFLECTION

Maria's story reminds us of the power of prayer. It is an example of God's heart toward us, and a demonstration of His power to change hearts and lives when we ask. It reminds us that our heavenly Father is faithful and eager to walk closely with us, and delights in our prayers.

The challenge then for each of us, as Paul writes, is to devote yourselves to prayer (Colossians 4:2); to pray continually (1 Thessalonians 5:17), and to be alert, and always praying (Ephesians 6:18) because we know the devil prowls around like a roaring lion seeking whom he may devour (1 Peter 5:8).

Prayer is power. May the prayer of our hearts be as the disciples, "Lord, teach us to pray" (Luke 11:1). We trust this book will help you grow in prayer as it continually strengthens your own personal walk with Jesus and those for whom you pray.

Let's continue to "approach God's throne of grace with confidence, so that we may receive mercy and find grace to help us in our time of need" (Hebrews 4:16). And "now may the grace of the Lord Jesus Christ, and the love of God, and the fellowship of the Holy Spirit be with you all" (2 Corinthians 13:14). Amen!

Note from the Author

In 2010, I began praying a prayer that transformed my prayer life. Dr. Jerry Kirk was speaking on the Lordship of Jesus Christ. "Each morning I pray, 'Dear Heavenly Father, thank You for Your grace that has made me Your dearly loved child.'" As he spoke of the surpassing love of God, his sermon inspired, equipped, and challenged me to pray the very prayer that empowered his ministry for over five decades because it was continually transforming him. This pastor, who had spent time with the Pope, Mother Teresa, and Billy Graham, was still being transformed into the image of Christ? I was intrigued.

At the conclusion of his sermon, Jerry invited the congregation to enter into a covenant prayer partnership with him. He said, "If you pray for me for thirty days by name, I will do the same for you." More than five hundred accepted his invitation.

That was the beginning of my life-changing journey of prayer. My husband and I began praying through the ten themes of that prayer, and I can honestly say we began receiving immediate results. It was amazing. I began to notice that when I didn't start my day with this simple prayer of commitment, I was not receiving the same opportunities to be a channel of His love and grace to those around me.

At that time, I had been serving as a children's choir

director at our church, serving in children's ministry for over twenty-five years. Although I loved Jesus, our family, our church, serving, and hospitality, I wanted more. I wanted to be used by God in powerful ways. I wanted to love Him more, serve Him more, and feel His presence tangibly. And I was willing to do whatever it took to make that happen.

I had been praying this prayer for three years when God gave me a vision of a children's prayer card. I called Jerry and asked if he had thought about putting the prayer into simple language that would speak to a child's heart. He asked me to assemble a team of educators that would work with his team. Five months later, we had a children's prayer card. I was then asked to write a book that would take pastors, teachers, and parents through the Prayer Covenant for Children. I had no idea where God was going to take it; but because of His grace, millions of children throughout the world have been impacted with this simple prayer tool—learning to love God, to pray, and to teach their friends to do the same.

God doesn't need us to accomplish His purposes, but He loves to accomplish His purposes in and through us. We don't have to be a pastor, teacher, leader, or theologian. In fact, the more you read through the Bible, the more you see how He chose insignificant, sometimes nameless individuals who simply stepped out in faith and followed in obedience.

Part of what transformed my prayer life was learning

to pray Jesus' prayers for myself and for whomever I prayed. When I intentionally pray the will of God over myself and someone else, He shows up fast and He shows up powerfully.

As we have watched the Prayer Covenant for Children spread throughout the globe, requests came to me several times for the creation of a Prayer Covenant for women. The first request was from my dear friend Anuja Lal. She and her husband, Deepak, served with Campus Crusade for Christ as directors of North India for over seven years before obeying God's call to venture out on their own and begin a church planting ministry in northern India. It has been amazing for me to watch their influence and impact grow over the decades and to see the fruit of their labor. All this is possible through God alone, working through willing, obedient, loving, compassionate, committed servants of Jesus.

When Anuja suggested writing a special prayer to speak to the hearts of women, to meet their spiritual and emotional needs, the idea made a lasting impression on me. It has taken several years to be able to sit down and begin writing. But God's timing is perfect, and I heard Him say, "It is time." *He Hears Her Voice* is the result of that season.

ACKNOWLEDGMENTS

HEARTFELT THANKS TO...

My wonderful husband and children for their constant support of the ministry.

My dear friend Anuja Lal, for suggesting the need for The Prayer Covenant, helping write the prayer and some of the questions.

Barbara Hayes for her insight and invaluable help with editing this book.

My precious daughter, Maria, for her encouragement, insight, and grammatical edits.

Ann Busch for her professional edits.

Tom Victor for his friendship, advocacy, and constant encouragement.

Carol Pecaitis for her guidance, support, and time invested in reviewing this resource.

All the women who submitted their powerful testimonies: Anuja Lal, Alexandra Richards, Barbara Hayes, Carol Pecaitis, Maria Marballi, Katie Steele, and Tim and Naomi Gillette. Your contributions enriched this book.

Stephen Eyre, for doing a theological review of the work.

The worship team at Saddleback for contributing their

amazing praise and worship songs to this project. Links to their music can be found here:

www.youtube.com/user/SaddlebackWorship
www.facebook.com/sbworship/
https://twitter.com/svccworship
www.saddlebackworship.com/music

Our wonderful Prayer Covenant team that serve faithfully day in and day out for the sake of the Gospel.

RESOURCES

CHAPTER 1

"Grace." *Merriam-Webster.com*. Merriam-Webster, 2020. Web. 25 June 2020. Merriam-Webster Online Dictionary copyright © 2015 by Merriam-Webster, Incorporated.

Saddleback Worship. "Room at the Table." *Matchless,* InResponse Music, 2017.

CHAPTER 2

"Love." *Merriam-Webster.com*. Merriam-Webster, 2020. Web. 25 June 2020. Merriam-Webster Online Dictionary copyright © 2015 by Merriam-Webster, Incorporated.

Featherson, William R. "My Jesus, I Love Thee." Public Domain, 1864.

Mother Teresa. *No Greater Love.* Servant Publications, Inc., 1997.

CHAPTER 3

"Compassion." *Merriam-Webster.com*. Merriam-Webster, 2020. Web. 25 June 2020. Merriam-Webster Online Dictionary copyright © 2015 by Merriam-Webster, Incorporated.

Chisholm, Thomas. "Great Is Thy Faithfulness." Public Domain, 1923.

CHAPTER 4

"Repentance." *Merriam-Webster.com*. Merriam-Webster, 2020. Web. 25 June 2020. Merriam-Webster Online Dictionary copyright © 2015 by Merriam-Webster, Incorporated.

Boom, Corrie ten. *Reflections of God's Glory.* Zondervan, 1999.

Elliott, Charlotte. "Just As I Am." Public Domain, 1836.

Lewis, C.S. *Mere Christianity.* HarperCollins Publishers, 2017.

CHAPTER 5

"Worship." *Merriam-Webster.com*. Merriam-Webster, 2020. Web. 25 June 2020. Merriam-Webster Online Dictionary copyright © 2015 by Merriam-Webster, Incorporated.

Thomas, Ken. "Praise God from Who All Blessings Flow." Public Domain, 1674.

CHAPTER 6

"Commitment." *Merriam-Webster.com*. Merriam-Webster, 2020. Web. 25 June 2020. Merriam-Webster Online Dictionary copyright © 2015 by Merriam-Webster, Incorporated.

Saddleback Worship. "Always Jesus." *Always Jesus,* The Fuel Music, 2019.

Mother Teresa. *No Greater Love.* Servant Publications, Inc., 1997.

CHAPTER 7

"Dependence." Merriam-Webster.com. Merriam-Webster, 2020. Web. 25 June 2020. Merriam-Webster Online Dictionary copyright © 2015 by Merriam-Webster, Incorporated.

Saddleback Worship. "Spirit of God." *Matchless*, InResponse Music, 2017.

CHAPTER 8

"Influence." *Merriam-Webster.com*. Merriam-Webster, 2020. Web. 25 June 2020. Merriam-Webster Online Dictionary copyright © 2015 by Merriam-Webster, Incorporated.

Book of Common Prayer According to the Use in King's Chapel. Oxford University Press, 1986.

Havergal, Frances R. "Take My Life and Let It Be." Public Domain, 1874.

CHAPTER 9

"Discipleship." *Dictionary.com*. Dictionary, 2021. Web. 2 July 2021. Copyright © 2021 Dictionary.com, LLC.

Saddleback Worship. "We Must Go." *We Must Go*, The Fuel Music, 2019.

CHAPTER 10

"Authority." Merriam-Webster.com. Merriam-Webster, 2020. Web. 25 June 2020. Merriam-Webster Online Dictionary copyright © 2015 by Merriam-Webster, Incorporated.

Perronet, Edward. "All Hail the Power of Jesus' Name." Public Domain, 1779.

About the Author

Candy Marballi, president and CEO of The Prayer Covenant, has served in children's ministries for over thirty years in the United States, Japan, and the Philippines. In addition to serving on the International Prayer Council and on the boards of The Great Commission Coalition and The Prayer Covenant, she hosts Teach Us to Pray each weekday on KARI 55 and The Prayer Covenant podcast weekly with Charisma Media. She is a wife of thirty-nine years to Vik Marballi, and they have two married children. They reside in New Albany, Ohio.

Her book, *The Prayer Covenant for Children*, was awarded the GOLD for Education award by Illumination Book Awards in 2015 and is presently being used to disciple, transform, and evangelize children and youth in seventy countries throughout Africa, Asia, Latin America, North America, and the Middle East. Over seven million children and youth have been reached with this prayer tool. She experienced the power of prayer at an early age. Her ministry and writing were shaped by a struggle with religious legalism in her childhood. Candy has a passion to make known God's gracious, accepting welcome extended through Jesus Christ.